C-3725 CAREER EXAMINATION SERIES

This is your
PASSBOOK for...

Income Maintenance Worker

Test Preparation Study Guide
Questions & Answers

COPYRIGHT NOTICE

This book is SOLELY intended for, is sold ONLY to, and its use is RESTRICTED to individual, bona fide applicants or candidates who qualify by virtue of having seriously filed applications for appropriate license, certificate, professional and/or promotional advancement, higher school matriculation, scholarship, or other legitimate requirements of education and/or governmental authorities.

This book is NOT intended for use, class instruction, tutoring, training, duplication, copying, reprinting, excerption, or adaptation, etc., by:

1) Other publishers
2) Proprietors and/or Instructors of "Coaching" and/or Preparatory Courses
3) Personnel and/or Training Divisions of commercial, industrial, and governmental organizations
4) Schools, colleges, or universities and/or their departments and staffs, including teachers and other personnel
5) Testing Agencies or Bureaus
6) Study groups which seek by the purchase of a single volume to copy and/or duplicate and/or adapt this material for use by the group as a whole without having purchased individual volumes for each of the members of the group
7) Et al.

Such persons would be in violation of appropriate Federal and State statutes.

PROVISION OF LICENSING AGREEMENTS – Recognized educational, commercial, industrial, and governmental institutions and organizations, and others legitimately engaged in educational pursuits, including training, testing, and measurement activities, may address request for a licensing agreement to the copyright owners, who will determine whether, and under what conditions, including fees and charges, the materials in this book may be used them. In other words, a licensing facility exists for the legitimate use of the material in this book on other than an individual basis. However, it is asseverated and affirmed here that the material in this book CANNOT be used without the receipt of the express permission of such a licensing agreement from the Publishers. Inquiries re licensing should be addressed to the company, attention rights and permissions department.

All rights reserved, including the right of reproduction in whole or in part, in any form or by any means, electronic or mechanical, including photocopying, recording, or by any information storage and retrieval system, without permission in writing from the Publisher.

Copyright © 2025 by
National Learning Corporation

212 Michael Drive, Syosset, NY 11791
(516) 921-8888 • www.passbooks.com
E-mail: info@passbooks.com

PASSBOOK® SERIES

THE *PASSBOOK® SERIES* has been created to prepare applicants and candidates for the ultimate academic battlefield – the examination room.

At some time in our lives, each and every one of us may be required to take an examination – for validation, matriculation, admission, qualification, registration, certification, or licensure.

Based on the assumption that every applicant or candidate has met the basic formal educational standards, has taken the required number of courses, and read the necessary texts, the *PASSBOOK® SERIES* furnishes the one special preparation which may assure passing with confidence, instead of failing with insecurity. Examination questions – together with answers – are furnished as the basic vehicle for study so that the mysteries of the examination and its compounding difficulties may be eliminated or diminished by a sure method.

This book is meant to help you pass your examination provided that you qualify and are serious in your objective.

The entire field is reviewed through the huge store of content information which is succinctly presented through a provocative and challenging approach – the question-and-answer method.

A climate of success is established by furnishing the correct answers at the end of each test.

You soon learn to recognize types of questions, forms of questions, and patterns of questioning. You may even begin to anticipate expected outcomes.

You perceive that many questions are repeated or adapted so that you can gain acute insights, which may enable you to score many sure points.

You learn how to confront new questions, or types of questions, and to attack them confidently and work out the correct answers.

You note objectives and emphases, and recognize pitfalls and dangers, so that you may make positive educational adjustments.

Moreover, you are kept fully informed in relation to new concepts, methods, practices, and directions in the field.

You discover that you are actually taking the examination all the time: you are preparing for the examination by "taking" an examination, not by reading extraneous and/or supererogatory textbooks.

In short, this PASSBOOK®, used directedly, should be an important factor in helping you to pass your test.

INCOME MAINTENANCE WORKER

DUTIES
Employees participate in classroom and on-the-job training to learn Department of Public Welfare procedures for determining if applicants meet the requirements for assistance. Employees also learn the requirements for programs such as Medical Assistance, Food Stamps, aid to Families with Dependent Children, etc. Under supervision, they interview persons applying for financial help and determine the assistance programs for which applicants qualify.

SCOPE OF THE WRITTEN TEST
The multiple-choice written test will cover knowledge, skills, and/or abilities in such areas as:
1. Income maintenance casework;
2. Interviewing techniques;
3. Computing benefits/income maintenance;
4. Completing forms; and
5. Interpretation of written materials.

HOW TO TAKE A TEST

I. YOU MUST PASS AN EXAMINATION

A. WHAT EVERY CANDIDATE SHOULD KNOW

Examination applicants often ask us for help in preparing for the written test. What can I study in advance? What kinds of questions will be asked? How will the test be given? How will the papers be graded?

As an applicant for a civil service examination, you may be wondering about some of these things. Our purpose here is to suggest effective methods of advance study and to describe civil service examinations.

Your chances for success on this examination can be increased if you know how to prepare. Those "pre-examination jitters" can be reduced if you know what to expect. You can even experience an adventure in good citizenship if you know why civil service exams are given.

B. WHY ARE CIVIL SERVICE EXAMINATIONS GIVEN?

Civil service examinations are important to you in two ways. As a citizen, you want public jobs filled by employees who know how to do their work. As a job seeker, you want a fair chance to compete for that job on an equal footing with other candidates. The best-known means of accomplishing this two-fold goal is the competitive examination.

Exams are widely publicized throughout the nation. They may be administered for jobs in federal, state, city, municipal, town or village governments or agencies.

Any citizen may apply, with some limitations, such as the age or residence of applicants. Your experience and education may be reviewed to see whether you meet the requirements for the particular examination. When these requirements exist, they are reasonable and applied consistently to all applicants. Thus, a competitive examination may cause you some uneasiness now, but it is your privilege and safeguard.

C. HOW ARE CIVIL SERVICE EXAMS DEVELOPED?

Examinations are carefully written by trained technicians who are specialists in the field known as "psychological measurement," in consultation with recognized authorities in the field of work that the test will cover. These experts recommend the subject matter areas or skills to be tested; only those knowledges or skills important to your success on the job are included. The most reliable books and source materials available are used as references. Together, the experts and technicians judge the difficulty level of the questions.

Test technicians know how to phrase questions so that the problem is clearly stated. Their ethics do not permit "trick" or "catch" questions. Questions may have been tried out on sample groups, or subjected to statistical analysis, to determine their usefulness.

Written tests are often used in combination with performance tests, ratings of training and experience, and oral interviews. All of these measures combine to form the best-known means of finding the right person for the right job.

II. HOW TO PASS THE WRITTEN TEST

A. NATURE OF THE EXAMINATION

To prepare intelligently for civil service examinations, you should know how they differ from school examinations you have taken. In school you were assigned certain definite pages to read or subjects to cover. The examination questions were quite detailed and usually emphasized memory. Civil service exams, on the other hand, try to discover your present ability to perform the duties of a position, plus your potentiality to learn these duties. In other words, a civil service exam attempts to predict how successful you will be. Questions cover such a broad area that they cannot be as minute and detailed as school exam questions.

In the public service similar kinds of work, or positions, are grouped together in one "class." This process is known as *position-classification*. All the positions in a class are paid according to the salary range for that class. One class title covers all of these positions, and they are all tested by the same examination.

B. FOUR BASIC STEPS

1) Study the announcement

How, then, can you know what subjects to study? Our best answer is: "Learn as much as possible about the class of positions for which you've applied." The exam will test the knowledge, skills and abilities needed to do the work.

Your most valuable source of information about the position you want is the official exam announcement. This announcement lists the training and experience qualifications. Check these standards and apply only if you come reasonably close to meeting them.

The brief description of the position in the examination announcement offers some clues to the subjects which will be tested. Think about the job itself. Review the duties in your mind. Can you perform them, or are there some in which you are rusty? Fill in the blank spots in your preparation.

Many jurisdictions preview the written test in the exam announcement by including a section called "Knowledge and Abilities Required," "Scope of the Examination," or some similar heading. Here you will find out specifically what fields will be tested.

2) Review your own background

Once you learn in general what the position is all about, and what you need to know to do the work, ask yourself which subjects you already know fairly well and which need improvement. You may wonder whether to concentrate on improving your strong areas or on building some background in your fields of weakness. When the announcement has specified "some knowledge" or "considerable knowledge," or has used adjectives like "beginning principles of..." or "advanced ... methods," you can get a clue as to the number and difficulty of questions to be asked in any given field. More questions, and hence broader coverage, would be included for those subjects which are more important in the work. Now weigh your strengths and weaknesses against the job requirements and prepare accordingly.

3) Determine the level of the position

Another way to tell how intensively you should prepare is to understand the level of the job for which you are applying. Is it the entering level? In other words, is this the position in which beginners in a field of work are hired? Or is it an intermediate or advanced level? Sometimes this is indicated by such words as "Junior" or "Senior" in the class title. Other jurisdictions use Roman numerals to designate the level – Clerk I, Clerk II, for example. The word "Supervisor" sometimes appears in the title. If the level is not indicated by the title, check the description of duties. Will you be working under very close supervision, or will you have responsibility for independent decisions in this work?

4) Choose appropriate study materials

Now that you know the subjects to be examined and the relative amount of each subject to be covered, you can choose suitable study materials. For beginning level jobs, or even advanced ones, if you have a pronounced weakness in some aspect of your training, read a modern, standard textbook in that field. Be sure it is up to date and has general coverage. Such books are normally available at your library, and the librarian will be glad to help you locate one. For entry-level positions, questions of appropriate difficulty are chosen – neither highly advanced questions, nor those too simple. Such questions require careful thought but not advanced training.

If the position for which you are applying is technical or advanced, you will read more advanced, specialized material. If you are already familiar with the basic principles of your field, elementary textbooks would waste your time. Concentrate on advanced textbooks and technical periodicals. Think through the concepts and review difficult problems in your field.

These are all general sources. You can get more ideas on your own initiative, following these leads. For example, training manuals and publications of the government agency which employs workers in your field can be useful, particularly for technical and professional positions. A letter or visit to the government department involved may result in more specific study suggestions, and certainly will provide you with a more definite idea of the exact nature of the position you are seeking.

III. KINDS OF TESTS

Tests are used for purposes other than measuring knowledge and ability to perform specified duties. For some positions, it is equally important to test ability to make adjustments to new situations or to profit from training. In others, basic mental abilities not dependent on information are essential. Questions which test these things may not appear as pertinent to the duties of the position as those which test for knowledge and information. Yet they are often highly important parts of a fair examination. For very general questions, it is almost impossible to help you direct your study efforts. What we can do is to point out some of the more common of these general abilities needed in public service positions and describe some typical questions.

1) General information

Broad, general information has been found useful for predicting job success in some kinds of work. This is tested in a variety of ways, from vocabulary lists to questions about current events. Basic background in some field of work, such as sociology or economics, may be sampled in a group of questions. Often these are principles which have become familiar to most persons through exposure rather than through formal training. It is difficult to advise you how to study for these questions; being alert to the world around you is our best suggestion.

2) Verbal ability

An example of an ability needed in many positions is verbal or language ability. Verbal ability is, in brief, the ability to use and understand words. Vocabulary and grammar tests are typical measures of this ability. Reading comprehension or paragraph interpretation questions are common in many kinds of civil service tests. You are given a paragraph of written material and asked to find its central meaning.

3) Numerical ability

Number skills can be tested by the familiar arithmetic problem, by checking paired lists of numbers to see which are alike and which are different, or by interpreting charts and graphs. In the latter test, a graph may be printed in the test booklet which you are asked to use as the basis for answering questions.

4) Observation

A popular test for law-enforcement positions is the observation test. A picture is shown to you for several minutes, then taken away. Questions about the picture test your ability to observe both details and larger elements.

5) Following directions

In many positions in the public service, the employee must be able to carry out written instructions dependably and accurately. You may be given a chart with several columns, each column listing a variety of information. The questions require you to carry out directions involving the information given in the chart.

6) Skills and aptitudes

Performance tests effectively measure some manual skills and aptitudes. When the skill is one in which you are trained, such as typing or shorthand, you can practice. These tests are often very much like those given in business school or high school courses. For many of the other skills and aptitudes, however, no short-time preparation can be made. Skills and abilities natural to you or that you have developed throughout your lifetime are being tested.

Many of the general questions just described provide all the data needed to answer the questions and ask you to use your reasoning ability to find the answers. Your best preparation for these tests, as well as for tests of facts and ideas, is to be at your physical and mental best. You, no doubt, have your own methods of getting into an exam-taking mood and keeping "in shape." The next section lists some ideas on this subject.

IV. KINDS OF QUESTIONS

Only rarely is the "essay" question, which you answer in narrative form, used in civil service tests. Civil service tests are usually of the short-answer type. Full instructions for answering these questions will be given to you at the examination. But in case this is your first experience with short-answer questions and separate answer sheets, here is what you need to know:

1) Multiple-choice Questions

Most popular of the short-answer questions is the "multiple choice" or "best answer" question. It can be used, for example, to test for factual knowledge, ability to solve problems or judgment in meeting situations found at work.

A multiple-choice question is normally one of three types—
- It can begin with an incomplete statement followed by several possible endings. You are to find the one ending which *best* completes the statement, although some of the others may not be entirely wrong.
- It can also be a complete statement in the form of a question which is answered by choosing one of the statements listed.

- It can be in the form of a problem – again you select the best answer.

Here is an example of a multiple-choice question with a discussion which should give you some clues as to the method for choosing the right answer:

When an employee has a complaint about his assignment, the action which will *best* help him overcome his difficulty is to
- A. discuss his difficulty with his coworkers
- B. take the problem to the head of the organization
- C. take the problem to the person who gave him the assignment
- D. say nothing to anyone about his complaint

In answering this question, you should study each of the choices to find which is best. Consider choice "A" – Certainly an employee may discuss his complaint with fellow employees, but no change or improvement can result, and the complaint remains unresolved. Choice "B" is a poor choice since the head of the organization probably does not know what assignment you have been given, and taking your problem to him is known as "going over the head" of the supervisor. The supervisor, or person who made the assignment, is the person who can clarify it or correct any injustice. Choice "C" is, therefore, correct. To say nothing, as in choice "D," is unwise. Supervisors have and interest in knowing the problems employees are facing, and the employee is seeking a solution to his problem.

2) True/False Questions

The "true/false" or "right/wrong" form of question is sometimes used. Here a complete statement is given. Your job is to decide whether the statement is right or wrong.

SAMPLE: A roaming cell-phone call to a nearby city costs less than a non-roaming call to a distant city.

This statement is wrong, or false, since roaming calls are more expensive.

This is not a complete list of all possible question forms, although most of the others are variations of these common types. You will always get complete directions for answering questions. Be sure you understand *how* to mark your answers – ask questions until you do.

V. RECORDING YOUR ANSWERS

Computer terminals are used more and more today for many different kinds of exams.

For an examination with very few applicants, you may be told to record your answers in the test booklet itself. Separate answer sheets are much more common. If this separate answer sheet is to be scored by machine – and this is often the case – it is highly important that you mark your answers correctly in order to get credit.

An electronic scoring machine is often used in civil service offices because of the speed with which papers can be scored. Machine-scored answer sheets must be marked with a pencil, which will be given to you. This pencil has a high graphite content which responds to the electronic scoring machine. As a matter of fact, stray dots may register as answers, so do not let your pencil rest on the answer sheet while you are pondering the correct answer. Also, if your pencil lead breaks or is otherwise defective, ask for another.

Since the answer sheet will be dropped in a slot in the scoring machine, be careful not to bend the corners or get the paper crumpled.

The answer sheet normally has five vertical columns of numbers, with 30 numbers to a column. These numbers correspond to the question numbers in your test booklet. After each number, going across the page are four or five pairs of dotted lines. These short dotted lines have small letters or numbers above them. The first two pairs may also have a "T" or "F" above the letters. This indicates that the first two pairs only are to be used if the questions are of the true-false type. If the questions are multiple choice, disregard the "T" and "F" and pay attention only to the small letters or numbers.

Answer your questions in the manner of the sample that follows:

32. The largest city in the United States is
    A. Washington, D.C.
    B. New York City
    C. Chicago
    D. Detroit
    E. San Francisco

1) Choose the answer you think is best. (New York City is the largest, so "B" is correct.)
2) Find the row of dotted lines numbered the same as the question you are answering. (Find row number 32)
3) Find the pair of dotted lines corresponding to the answer. (Find the pair of lines under the mark "B.")
4) Make a solid black mark between the dotted lines.

VI. BEFORE THE TEST

Common sense will help you find procedures to follow to get ready for an examination. Too many of us, however, overlook these sensible measures. Indeed, nervousness and fatigue have been found to be the most serious reasons why applicants fail to do their best on civil service tests. Here is a list of reminders:

- Begin your preparation early – Don't wait until the last minute to go scurrying around for books and materials or to find out what the position is all about.
- Prepare continuously – An hour a night for a week is better than an all-night cram session. This has been definitely established. What is more, a night a week for a month will return better dividends than crowding your study into a shorter period of time.
- Locate the place of the exam – You have been sent a notice telling you when and where to report for the examination. If the location is in a different town or otherwise unfamiliar to you, it would be well to inquire the best route and learn something about the building.
- Relax the night before the test – Allow your mind to rest. Do not study at all that night. Plan some mild recreation or diversion; then go to bed early and get a good night's sleep.
- Get up early enough to make a leisurely trip to the place for the test – This way unforeseen events, traffic snarls, unfamiliar buildings, etc. will not upset you.
- Dress comfortably – A written test is not a fashion show. You will be known by number and not by name, so wear something comfortable.

- Leave excess paraphernalia at home – Shopping bags and odd bundles will get in your way. You need bring only the items mentioned in the official notice you received; usually everything you need is provided. Do not bring reference books to the exam. They will only confuse those last minutes and be taken away from you when in the test room.
- Arrive somewhat ahead of time – If because of transportation schedules you must get there very early, bring a newspaper or magazine to take your mind off yourself while waiting.
- Locate the examination room – When you have found the proper room, you will be directed to the seat or part of the room where you will sit. Sometimes you are given a sheet of instructions to read while you are waiting. Do not fill out any forms until you are told to do so; just read them and be prepared.
- Relax and prepare to listen to the instructions
- If you have any physical problem that may keep you from doing your best, be sure to tell the test administrator. If you are sick or in poor health, you really cannot do your best on the exam. You can come back and take the test some other time.

VII. AT THE TEST

The day of the test is here and you have the test booklet in your hand. The temptation to get going is very strong. Caution! There is more to success than knowing the right answers. You must know how to identify your papers and understand variations in the type of short-answer question used in this particular examination. Follow these suggestions for maximum results from your efforts:

1) Cooperate with the monitor

The test administrator has a duty to create a situation in which you can be as much at ease as possible. He will give instructions, tell you when to begin, check to see that you are marking your answer sheet correctly, and so on. He is not there to guard you, although he will see that your competitors do not take unfair advantage. He wants to help you do your best.

2) Listen to all instructions

Don't jump the gun! Wait until you understand all directions. In most civil service tests you get more time than you need to answer the questions. So don't be in a hurry. Read each word of instructions until you clearly understand the meaning. Study the examples, listen to all announcements and follow directions. Ask questions if you do not understand what to do.

3) Identify your papers

Civil service exams are usually identified by number only. You will be assigned a number; you must not put your name on your test papers. Be sure to copy your number correctly. Since more than one exam may be given, copy your exact examination title.

4) Plan your time

Unless you are told that a test is a "speed" or "rate of work" test, speed itself is usually not important. Time enough to answer all the questions will be provided, but this does not mean that you have all day. An overall time limit has been set. Divide the total time (in minutes) by the number of questions to determine the approximate time you have for each question.

5) Do not linger over difficult questions

If you come across a difficult question, mark it with a paper clip (useful to have along) and come back to it when you have been through the booklet. One caution if you do this – be sure to skip a number on your answer sheet as well. Check often to be sure that you have not lost your place and that you are marking in the row numbered the same as the question you are answering.

6) Read the questions

Be sure you know what the question asks! Many capable people are unsuccessful because they failed to *read* the questions correctly.

7) Answer all questions

Unless you have been instructed that a penalty will be deducted for incorrect answers, it is better to guess than to omit a question.

8) Speed tests

It is often better NOT to guess on speed tests. It has been found that on timed tests people are tempted to spend the last few seconds before time is called in marking answers at random – without even reading them – in the hope of picking up a few extra points. To discourage this practice, the instructions may warn you that your score will be "corrected" for guessing. That is, a penalty will be applied. The incorrect answers will be deducted from the correct ones, or some other penalty formula will be used.

9) Review your answers

If you finish before time is called, go back to the questions you guessed or omitted to give them further thought. Review other answers if you have time.

10) Return your test materials

If you are ready to leave before others have finished or time is called, take ALL your materials to the monitor and leave quietly. Never take any test material with you. The monitor can discover whose papers are not complete, and taking a test booklet may be grounds for disqualification.

VIII. EXAMINATION TECHNIQUES

1) Read the general instructions carefully. These are usually printed on the first page of the exam booklet. As a rule, these instructions refer to the timing of the examination; the fact that you should not start work until the signal and must stop work at a signal, etc. If there are any *special* instructions, such as a choice of questions to be answered, make sure that you note this instruction carefully.

2) When you are ready to start work on the examination, that is as soon as the signal has been given, read the instructions to each question booklet, underline any key words or phrases, such as *least, best, outline, describe* and the like. In this way you will tend to answer as requested rather than discover on reviewing your paper that you *listed without describing*, that you selected the *worst* choice rather than the *best* choice, etc.

3) If the examination is of the objective or multiple-choice type – that is, each question will also give a series of possible answers: A, B, C or D, and you are called upon to select the best answer and write the letter next to that answer on your answer paper – it is advisable to start answering each question in turn. There may be anywhere from 50 to 100 such questions in the three or four hours allotted and you can see how much time would be taken if you read through all the questions before beginning to answer any. Furthermore, if you come across a question or group of questions which you know would be difficult to answer, it would undoubtedly affect your handling of all the other questions.

4) If the examination is of the essay type and contains but a few questions, it is a moot point as to whether you should read all the questions before starting to answer any one. Of course, if you are given a choice – say five out of seven and the like – then it is essential to read all the questions so you can eliminate the two that are most difficult. If, however, you are asked to answer all the questions, there may be danger in trying to answer the easiest one first because you may find that you will spend too much time on it. The best technique is to answer the first question, then proceed to the second, etc.

5) Time your answers. Before the exam begins, write down the time it started, then add the time allowed for the examination and write down the time it must be completed, then divide the time available somewhat as follows:
   - If 3-1/2 hours are allowed, that would be 210 minutes. If you have 80 objective-type questions, that would be an average of 2-1/2 minutes per question. Allow yourself no more than 2 minutes per question, or a total of 160 minutes, which will permit about 50 minutes to review.
   - If for the time allotment of 210 minutes there are 7 essay questions to answer, that would average about 30 minutes a question. Give yourself only 25 minutes per question so that you have about 35 minutes to review.

6) The most important instruction is to *read each question* and make sure you know what is wanted. The second most important instruction is to *time yourself properly* so that you answer every question. The third most important instruction is to *answer every question*. Guess if you have to but include something for each question. Remember that you will receive no credit for a blank and will probably receive some credit if you write something in answer to an essay question. If you guess a letter – say "B" for a multiple-choice question – you may have guessed right. If you leave a blank as an answer to a multiple-choice question, the examiners may respect your feelings but it will not add a point to your score. Some exams may penalize you for wrong answers, so in such cases *only*, you may not want to guess unless you have some basis for your answer.

7) Suggestions
   a. Objective-type questions
      1. Examine the question booklet for proper sequence of pages and questions
      2. Read all instructions carefully
      3. Skip any question which seems too difficult; return to it after all other questions have been answered
      4. Apportion your time properly; do not spend too much time on any single question or group of questions

5. Note and underline key words – *all, most, fewest, least, best, worst, same, opposite,* etc.
6. Pay particular attention to negatives
7. Note unusual option, e.g., unduly long, short, complex, different or similar in content to the body of the question
8. Observe the use of "hedging" words – *probably, may, most likely,* etc.
9. Make sure that your answer is put next to the same number as the question
10. Do not second-guess unless you have good reason to believe the second answer is definitely more correct
11. Cross out original answer if you decide another answer is more accurate; do not erase until you are ready to hand your paper in
12. Answer all questions; guess unless instructed otherwise
13. Leave time for review

   b. Essay questions
     1. Read each question carefully
     2. Determine exactly what is wanted. Underline key words or phrases.
     3. Decide on outline or paragraph answer
     4. Include many different points and elements unless asked to develop any one or two points or elements
     5. Show impartiality by giving pros and cons unless directed to select one side only
     6. Make and write down any assumptions you find necessary to answer the questions
     7. Watch your English, grammar, punctuation and choice of words
     8. Time your answers; don't crowd material

8) Answering the essay question

Most essay questions can be answered by framing the specific response around several key words or ideas. Here are a few such key words or ideas:

M's: manpower, materials, methods, money, management
P's: purpose, program, policy, plan, procedure, practice, problems, pitfalls, personnel, public relations

   a. Six basic steps in handling problems:
     1. Preliminary plan and background development
     2. Collect information, data and facts
     3. Analyze and interpret information, data and facts
     4. Analyze and develop solutions as well as make recommendations
     5. Prepare report and sell recommendations
     6. Install recommendations and follow up effectiveness

   b. Pitfalls to avoid
     1. *Taking things for granted* – A statement of the situation does not necessarily imply that each of the elements is necessarily true; for example, a complaint may be invalid and biased so that all that can be taken for granted is that a complaint has been registered

2. *Considering only one side of a situation* – Wherever possible, indicate several alternatives and then point out the reasons you selected the best one
3. *Failing to indicate follow up* – Whenever your answer indicates action on your part, make certain that you will take proper follow-up action to see how successful your recommendations, procedures or actions turn out to be
4. *Taking too long in answering any single question* – Remember to time your answers properly

IX. AFTER THE TEST

Scoring procedures differ in detail among civil service jurisdictions although the general principles are the same. Whether the papers are hand-scored or graded by machine we have described, they are nearly always graded by number. That is, the person who marks the paper knows only the number – never the name – of the applicant. Not until all the papers have been graded will they be matched with names. If other tests, such as training and experience or oral interview ratings have been given, scores will be combined. Different parts of the examination usually have different weights. For example, the written test might count 60 percent of the final grade, and a rating of training and experience 40 percent. In many jurisdictions, veterans will have a certain number of points added to their grades.

After the final grade has been determined, the names are placed in grade order and an eligible list is established. There are various methods for resolving ties between those who get the same final grade – probably the most common is to place first the name of the person whose application was received first. Job offers are made from the eligible list in the order the names appear on it. You will be notified of your grade and your rank as soon as all these computations have been made. This will be done as rapidly as possible.

People who are found to meet the requirements in the announcement are called "eligibles." Their names are put on a list of eligible candidates. An eligible's chances of getting a job depend on how high he stands on this list and how fast agencies are filling jobs from the list.

When a job is to be filled from a list of eligibles, the agency asks for the names of people on the list of eligibles for that job. When the civil service commission receives this request, it sends to the agency the names of the three people highest on this list. Or, if the job to be filled has specialized requirements, the office sends the agency the names of the top three persons who meet these requirements from the general list.

The appointing officer makes a choice from among the three people whose names were sent to him. If the selected person accepts the appointment, the names of the others are put back on the list to be considered for future openings.

That is the rule in hiring from all kinds of eligible lists, whether they are for typist, carpenter, chemist, or something else. For every vacancy, the appointing officer has his choice of any one of the top three eligibles on the list. This explains why the person whose name is on top of the list sometimes does not get an appointment when some of the persons lower on the list do. If the appointing officer chooses the second or third eligible, the No. 1 eligible does not get a job at once, but stays on the list until he is appointed or the list is terminated.

X. HOW TO PASS THE INTERVIEW TEST

The examination for which you applied requires an oral interview test. You have already taken the written test and you are now being called for the interview test – the final part of the formal examination.

You may think that it is not possible to prepare for an interview test and that there are no procedures to follow during an interview. Our purpose is to point out some things you can do in advance that will help you and some good rules to follow and pitfalls to avoid while you are being interviewed.

What is an interview supposed to test?

The written examination is designed to test the technical knowledge and competence of the candidate; the oral is designed to evaluate intangible qualities, not readily measured otherwise, and to establish a list showing the relative fitness of each candidate – as measured against his competitors – for the position sought. Scoring is not on the basis of "right" and "wrong," but on a sliding scale of values ranging from "not passable" to "outstanding." As a matter of fact, it is possible to achieve a relatively low score without a single "incorrect" answer because of evident weakness in the qualities being measured.

Occasionally, an examination may consist entirely of an oral test – either an individual or a group oral. In such cases, information is sought concerning the technical knowledges and abilities of the candidate, since there has been no written examination for this purpose. More commonly, however, an oral test is used to supplement a written examination.

Who conducts interviews?

The composition of oral boards varies among different jurisdictions. In nearly all, a representative of the personnel department serves as chairman. One of the members of the board may be a representative of the department in which the candidate would work. In some cases, "outside experts" are used, and, frequently, a businessman or some other representative of the general public is asked to serve. Labor and management or other special groups may be represented. The aim is to secure the services of experts in the appropriate field.

However the board is composed, it is a good idea (and not at all improper or unethical) to ascertain in advance of the interview who the members are and what groups they represent. When you are introduced to them, you will have some idea of their backgrounds and interests, and at least you will not stutter and stammer over their names.

What should be done before the interview?

While knowledge about the board members is useful and takes some of the surprise element out of the interview, there is other preparation which is more substantive. It *is* possible to prepare for an oral interview – in several ways:

1) Keep a copy of your application and review it carefully before the interview

This may be the only document before the oral board, and the starting point of the interview. Know what education and experience you have listed there, and the sequence and dates of all of it. Sometimes the board will ask you to review the highlights of your experience for them; you should not have to hem and haw doing it.

2) Study the class specification and the examination announcement

Usually, the oral board has one or both of these to guide them. The qualities, characteristics or knowledges required by the position sought are stated in these documents. They offer valuable clues as to the nature of the oral interview. For example, if the job involves supervisory responsibilities, the announcement will usually indicate that knowledge of modern supervisory methods and the qualifications of the candidate as a supervisor will be tested. If so, you can expect such questions, frequently in the form of a hypothetical situation which you are expected to solve. NEVER go into an oral without knowledge of the duties and responsibilities of the job you seek.

3) Think through each qualification required

Try to visualize the kind of questions you would ask if you were a board member. How well could you answer them? Try especially to appraise your own knowledge and background in each area, *measured against the job sought*, and identify any areas in which you are weak. Be critical and realistic – do not flatter yourself.

4) Do some general reading in areas in which you feel you may be weak

For example, if the job involves supervision and your past experience has NOT, some general reading in supervisory methods and practices, particularly in the field of human relations, might be useful. Do NOT study agency procedures or detailed manuals. The oral board will be testing your understanding and capacity, not your memory.

5) Get a good night's sleep and watch your general health and mental attitude

You will want a clear head at the interview. Take care of a cold or any other minor ailment, and of course, no hangovers.

What should be done on the day of the interview?

Now comes the day of the interview itself. Give yourself plenty of time to get there. Plan to arrive somewhat ahead of the scheduled time, particularly if your appointment is in the fore part of the day. If a previous candidate fails to appear, the board might be ready for you a bit early. By early afternoon an oral board is almost invariably behind schedule if there are many candidates, and you may have to wait. Take along a book or magazine to read, or your application to review, but leave any extraneous material in the waiting room when you go in for your interview. In any event, relax and compose yourself.

The matter of dress is important. The board is forming impressions about you – from your experience, your manners, your attitude, and your appearance. Give your personal appearance careful attention. Dress your best, but not your flashiest. Choose conservative, appropriate clothing, and be sure it is immaculate. This is a business interview, and your appearance should indicate that you regard it as such. Besides, being well groomed and properly dressed will help boost your confidence.

Sooner or later, someone will call your name and escort you into the interview room. *This is it.* From here on you are on your own. It is too late for any more preparation. But remember, you asked for this opportunity to prove your fitness, and you are here because your request was granted.

What happens when you go in?

The usual sequence of events will be as follows: The clerk (who is often the board stenographer) will introduce you to the chairman of the oral board, who will introduce you to the other members of the board. Acknowledge the introductions before you sit down. Do not be surprised if you find a microphone facing you or a stenotypist sitting by. Oral interviews are usually recorded in the event of an appeal or other review.

Usually the chairman of the board will open the interview by reviewing the highlights of your education and work experience from your application – primarily for the benefit of the other members of the board, as well as to get the material into the record. Do not interrupt or comment unless there is an error or significant misinterpretation; if that is the case, do not hesitate. But do not quibble about insignificant matters. Also, he will usually ask you some question about your education, experience or your present job – partly to get you to start talking and to establish the interviewing "rapport." He may start the actual questioning, or turn it over to one of the other members. Frequently, each member undertakes the questioning on a particular area, one in which he is perhaps most competent, so you can expect each member to participate in the examination. Because time is limited, you may also expect some rather abrupt switches in the direction the questioning takes, so do not be upset by it. Normally, a board member will not pursue a single line of questioning unless he discovers a particular strength or weakness.

After each member has participated, the chairman will usually ask whether any member has any further questions, then will ask you if you have anything you wish to add. Unless you are expecting this question, it may floor you. Worse, it may start you off on an extended, extemporaneous speech. The board is not usually seeking more information. The question is principally to offer you a last opportunity to present further qualifications or to indicate that you have nothing to add. So, if you feel that a significant qualification or characteristic has been overlooked, it is proper to point it out in a sentence or so. Do not compliment the board on the thoroughness of their examination – they have been sketchy, and you know it. If you wish, merely say, "No thank you, I have nothing further to add." This is a point where you can "talk yourself out" of a good impression or fail to present an important bit of information. Remember, *you close the interview yourself.*

The chairman will then say, "That is all, Mr. _____, thank you." Do not be startled; the interview is over, and quicker than you think. Thank him, gather your belongings and take your leave. Save your sigh of relief for the other side of the door.

How to put your best foot forward

Throughout this entire process, you may feel that the board individually and collectively is trying to pierce your defenses, seek out your hidden weaknesses and embarrass and confuse you. Actually, this is not true. They are obliged to make an appraisal of your qualifications for the job you are seeking, and they want to see you in your best light. Remember, they must interview all candidates and a non-cooperative candidate may become a failure in spite of their best efforts to bring out his qualifications. Here are 15 suggestions that will help you:

1) Be natural – Keep your attitude confident, not cocky

If you are not confident that you can do the job, do not expect the board to be. Do not apologize for your weaknesses, try to bring out your strong points. The board is interested in a positive, not negative, presentation. Cockiness will antagonize any board member and make him wonder if you are covering up a weakness by a false show of strength.

2) Get comfortable, but don't lounge or sprawl

Sit erectly but not stiffly. A careless posture may lead the board to conclude that you are careless in other things, or at least that you are not impressed by the importance of the occasion. Either conclusion is natural, even if incorrect. Do not fuss with your clothing, a pencil or an ashtray. Your hands may occasionally be useful to emphasize a point; do not let them become a point of distraction.

3) Do not wisecrack or make small talk

This is a serious situation, and your attitude should show that you consider it as such. Further, the time of the board is limited – they do not want to waste it, and neither should you.

4) Do not exaggerate your experience or abilities

In the first place, from information in the application or other interviews and sources, the board may know more about you than you think. Secondly, you probably will not get away with it. An experienced board is rather adept at spotting such a situation, so do not take the chance.

5) If you know a board member, do not make a point of it, yet do not hide it

Certainly you are not fooling him, and probably not the other members of the board. Do not try to take advantage of your acquaintanceship – it will probably do you little good.

6) Do not dominate the interview

Let the board do that. They will give you the clues – do not assume that you have to do all the talking. Realize that the board has a number of questions to ask you, and do not try to take up all the interview time by showing off your extensive knowledge of the answer to the first one.

7) Be attentive

You only have 20 minutes or so, and you should keep your attention at its sharpest throughout. When a member is addressing a problem or question to you, give him your undivided attention. Address your reply principally to him, but do not exclude the other board members.

8) Do not interrupt

A board member may be stating a problem for you to analyze. He will ask you a question when the time comes. Let him state the problem, and wait for the question.

9) Make sure you understand the question

Do not try to answer until you are sure what the question is. If it is not clear, restate it in your own words or ask the board member to clarify it for you. However, do not haggle about minor elements.

10) Reply promptly but not hastily

A common entry on oral board rating sheets is "candidate responded readily," or "candidate hesitated in replies." Respond as promptly and quickly as you can, but do not jump to a hasty, ill-considered answer.

11) Do not be peremptory in your answers

A brief answer is proper – but do not fire your answer back. That is a losing game from your point of view. The board member can probably ask questions much faster than you can answer them.

12) Do not try to create the answer you think the board member wants

He is interested in what kind of mind you have and how it works – not in playing games. Furthermore, he can usually spot this practice and will actually grade you down on it.

13) Do not switch sides in your reply merely to agree with a board member

Frequently, a member will take a contrary position merely to draw you out and to see if you are willing and able to defend your point of view. Do not start a debate, yet do not surrender a good position. If a position is worth taking, it is worth defending.

14) Do not be afraid to admit an error in judgment if you are shown to be wrong

The board knows that you are forced to reply without any opportunity for careful consideration. Your answer may be demonstrably wrong. If so, admit it and get on with the interview.

15) Do not dwell at length on your present job

The opening question may relate to your present assignment. Answer the question but do not go into an extended discussion. You are being examined for a *new* job, not your present one. As a matter of fact, try to phrase ALL your answers in terms of the job for which you are being examined.

Basis of Rating

Probably you will forget most of these "do's" and "don'ts" when you walk into the oral interview room. Even remembering them all will not ensure you a passing grade. Perhaps you did not have the qualifications in the first place. But remembering them will help you to put your best foot forward, without treading on the toes of the board members.

Rumor and popular opinion to the contrary notwithstanding, an oral board wants you to make the best appearance possible. They know you are under pressure – but they also want to see how you respond to it as a guide to what your reaction would be under the pressures of the job you seek. They will be influenced by the degree of poise you display, the personal traits you show and the manner in which you respond.

ABOUT THIS BOOK

This book contains tests divided into Examination Sections. Go through each test, answering every question in the margin. We have also attached a sample answer sheet at the back of the book that can be removed and used. At the end of each test look at the answer key and check your answers. On the ones you got wrong, look at the right answer choice and learn. Do not fill in the answers first. Do not memorize the questions and answers, but understand the answer and principles involved. On your test, the questions will likely be different from the samples. Questions are changed and new ones added. If you understand these past questions you should have success with any changes that arise. Tests may consist of several types of questions. We have additional books on each subject should more study be advisable or necessary for you. Finally, the more you study, the better prepared you will be. This book is intended to be the last thing you study before you walk into the examination room. Prior study of relevant texts is also recommended. NLC publishes some of these in our Fundamental Series. Knowledge and good sense are important factors in passing your exam. Good luck also helps. So now study this Passbook, absorb the material contained within and take that knowledge into the examination. Then do your best to pass that exam.

EXAMINATION SECTION

EXAMINATION SECTION
TEST 1

DIRECTIONS: Each question or incomplete statement is followed by several suggested answers or completions. Select the one that BEST answers the question or completes the statement. *PRINT THE LETTER OF THE CORRECT ANSWER IN THE SPACE AT THE RIGHT.*

1. You find that an applicant for public assistance is hesitant about showing you some required personal material and documents. Your INITIAL reaction to this situation should be to

    A. quietly insist that he give you the required materials
    B. make an exception in his case to avoid making him uncomfortable
    C. suspect that he may be trying to withhold evidence
    D. understand that he is in a stressful situation and may feel ashamed to reveal such information

    1.____

2. An applicant has just given you a response which does not seem clear. Of the following, the BEST course of action for you to take in order to check your understanding of the applicant's response is for you to

    A. ask the question again during a subsequent interview with this applicant
    B. repeat the applicant's answer in the applicant.s own words and ask if that is what the applicant meant
    C. later in the interview, repeat the question that led to this response
    D. repeat the question that led to this response, but say it more forcefully

    2.____

3. While speaking with applicants for public assistance, you may find that there are times when an applicant will be silent for a short while before answering questions. In order to gather the BEST information from the applicant, the interviewer should *generally* treat these silences by

    A. repeating the same question to make the applicant stop hesitating
    B. rephrasing the question in a way that the applicant can answer it faster
    C. directing an easier question to the applicant so that he can gain confidence in answering
    D. waiting patiently and not pressuring the applicant into quick undeveloped answers

    3.____

4. In dealing with members of different ethnic and religious groups among the applicants you interview, you should give

    A. individuals the services to which they are entitled
    B. less service to those you judge to be more advantaged
    C. better service to groups with which you sympathize most
    D. better service to group with political *muscle*

    4.____

5. You must be sure that, when interviewing an applicant, you phrase each question carefully. Of the following, the MOST important reason for this is to insure that

    A. the applicant will phrase each of his responses carefully
    B. you use correct grammar
    C. it is clear to the applicant what information you are seeking
    D. you do not word the same question differently for different applicants

    5.____

1

6. When given a form to complete, a client hesitates, tells you that he cannot fill out forms too well, and that he is afraid he will do a poor job. He asks you to do it for him. You are quite sure, however, that he is able to do it himself. In this case, it would be MOST advisable for you to

   A. encourage him to try filling out the application as well as he can
   B. fill out the application for him
   C. explain to him that he must learn to accept responsibility
   D. tell him that, if others can fill out an application, he can too

7. Assume that an applicant for public assistance whom you are interviewing has made a statement that is obviously not true. Of the following, the BEST course of action for you to take at this point in the interview is to

   A. ask the applicant if he is sure about his statement
   B. tell the applicant that his statement is incorrect
   C. question the applicant further to clarify his response
   D. assume that the statement is true

8. Assume that you are conducting an initial interview with an applicant for public assistance. Of the following, the MOST advisable questions for you to ask at the beginning of this interview are questions that

   A. can be answered in one or two sentences
   B. have nothing to do with the subject matter of the interview
   C. are most likely to reveal any hostility on the part of the applicant
   D. the applicant is most likely to be willing and able to answer

9. When interviewing a particularly nervous and upset applicant for public assistance, the one of the following actions which you should take FIRST is to

   A. inform the applicant that, to be helped, he must cooperate
   B. advise the applicant that proof must be provided for statements he makes
   C. assure the applicant that every effort will be made to provide him with whatever assistance he is entitled to
   D. tell the applicant he will have no trouble obtaining public assistance so long as he is truthful

10. Assume that, following normal routine, it is part of your job to prepare a monthly report for your unit head that eventually goes to the Director of your Center. The report contains information on the number of applicants you have interviewed that have been approved for different types of public assistance and the number of applicants you have interviewed that have been turned down. Errors on such reports are *serious* because

    A. you are expected to be able to prove how many applicants you have interviewed each month
    B. accurate statistics are needed for effective management of the department
    C. they may not be discovered before the report is transmitted to the Center Director
    D. they may result in a loss of assistance to the applicants left out of the report

11. During interviews, people give information about themselves in several ways. Which of the following *usually* gives the LEAST amount of information about the person being questioned? His

    A. spoken words
    B. tone of voice
    C. facial expression
    D. body position

12. Suppose an applicant, while being interviewed about his eligibility for public assistance, becomes angered by your questioning and begins to use sharp, uncontrolled language. Which of the following is the BEST way for you to react to him?

    A. Speak in his style to show him that you are neither impressed nor upset by his speech
    B. Interrupt him and tell him that you are not required to listen to this kind of speech
    C. Lower your voice and slow the rate of your speech in an attempt to set an example that will calm him
    D. Let him continue in his way but insist that he answer your questions directly

13. You have been informed that no determination has yet been made on the eligibility of an applicant for public assistance. The decision depends on further checking. His situation, however, is similar to that of many other applicants whose eligibility has been approved. The applicant calls you, quite worried, and asks you whether his application has been accepted. What would be BEST for you to do under these circumstances? Tell him

    A. his application is being checked and you will let him know the final result as soon as possible
    B. that a written request addressed to your supervisor will probably get faster action for his case
    C. not to worry since other applicants with similar backgrounds have already been accepted
    D. since there is no definite information and you are very busy, you will call him back

14. Suppose that you have been talking with an applicant for public assistance. You have the feeling from the latest things the applicant has said that some of his answers to earlier questions were not totally correct. You guess that he might have been afraid or confused earlier but that your conversation has now put him in a more comfortable frame of mind. In order to test the reliability of information received from the earlier questions, the BEST thing for you to do *now* is to ask new questions that

    A. allow the applicant to explain why he deliberately gave false information to you
    B. ask for the same information, although worded differently from the original questions
    C. put pressure on the applicant so that he personally wants to clear up the facts in his earlier answers
    D. indicate to the applicant that you are aware of his deceptiveness

15. Assume that you are a supervisor. While providing you with required information, an applicant for public assistance informs you that she does not know who is the father of her child. Of the following, the MOST advisable action for you to take is to

    A. ask her to explain further
    B. advise her about birth control facilities
    C. express your sympathy for the situation
    D. go on to the next item of information

16. If, in an interview, you wish to determine a client's usual occupation, which one of the following questions is MOST likely to elicit the most useful information?

    A. Did you ever work in a factory?
    B. Do you know how to do office work?
    C. What kind of work do you do?
    D. Where are you working now?

17. Assume that, in the course of the day, you are approached by a clerk from another office who starts questioning you about one of the clients you have just interviewed. The clerk says that she is a relative of the client. According to departmental policy, all matters discussed with clients are to be kept confidential. Of the following, the BEST course of action for you to take in this situation would be to

    A. check to see whether the clerk is really a relative before you make any further decision
    B. explain to the clerk why you cannot divulge the information
    C. tell the clerk that you do not know the answers to her questions
    D. tell the clerk that she can get from the client any information the client wishes to give

18. Which of the following is *usually* the BEST technique for you, as an interviewer, to use to bring an applicant back to subject matter from which the applicant has strayed?

    A. Ask the applicant a question that is related to the subject of the interview
    B. Show the applicant that his response is unrelated to the question
    C. Discreetly remind the applicant that there is a time allotment for the interview
    D. Tell the applicant that you will be happy to discuss the extraneous matters at a future interview

19. Assume that you notice that one of the clerks has accidentally pulled the wrong form to give to her client. Of the following, the BEST way for you to handle this situation would be to tell

    A. the clerk about her error, and precisely describe the problems that will result
    B. the clerk about her error in an understanding and friendly way
    C. the clerk about her error in a humorous way and tell her that no real damage was done
    D. your supervisor that clerks need more training in the use and application of departmental forms

20. Of the following characteristics, the one which would be MOST valuable when helping an angry applicant to understand why he has received less assistance than he believes he is entitled to would be the ability to

    A. state the rules exactly as they apply to the applicant's problem
    B. cite examples of other cases where the results have been similar
    C. remain patient and understanding of the person's feelings
    D. remain completely objective and uninvolved in individual personal problems

21. Reports are usually divided into several sections, some of which are more necessary than others. Of the following, the section which is MOST often necessary to include in a report is a(n)

    A. table of contents
    B. introduction
    C. index
    D. bibliography

22. Suppose you are writing a report on an interview you have just completed with a particularly hostile applicant for public assistance. Which of the following BEST describes what you should include in this report?

    A. What you think caused the applicant.s hostile attitude during the interview
    B. Specific examples of the applicant.s hostile remarks and behavior
    C. The relevant information uncovered during the interview
    D. A recommendation that the applicant.s request be denied because of his hostility

23. When including recommendations in a report to your supervisor, which of the following is MOST important for you to do?

    A. Provide several alternative courses of action for each recommendation
    B. First present the supporting evidence, then the recommendations
    C. First present the recommendations, then the supporting evidence
    D. Make sure the recommendations arise logically out of the information in the report

24. It is often necessary that the writer of a report present facts and sufficient arguments to gain acceptance of the points, conclusions, or recommendations set forth in the report. Of the following, the LEAST advisable step to take in organizing a report, when such argumentation is the important factor, is a(n)

    A. elaborate expression of personal belief
    B. businesslike discussion of the problem as a whole
    C. orderly arrangement of convincing data
    D. reasonable explanation of the primary issues

25. Suppose you receive a phone call from an applicant about a problem which requires that you must look up the information and call her back. Although the applicant had given you her name earlier and you can pronounce the name, you are not sure that you can spell it correctly. Asking the applicant to spell her name is

    A. *good,* because this indicates to the applicant that you intend to obtain the information she requested
    B. *poor,* because she may feel you are making fun of her name
    C. *good,* because you will be sure to get the correct name
    D. *poor,* because she will think you have not been listening to her

KEY (CORRECT ANSWERS)

1. D
2. B
3. D
4. A
5. C

6. A
7. C
8. D
9. C
10. B

11. D
12. C
13. A
14. B
15. D

16. C
17. B
18. A
19. B
20. C

21. B
22. C
23. D
24. A
25. C

TEST 2

DIRECTIONS: Each question or incomplete statement is followed by several suggested answers or completions. Select the one that BEST answers the question or completes the statement. *PRINT THE LETTER OF THE CORRECT ANSWER IN THE SPACE AT THE RIGHT.*

Questions 1-9.

DIRECTIONS: Answer Questions 1 through 9 SOLELY on the basis of the information in the following passage.

The establishment of a procedure whereby the client's rent is paid directly by the Social Service agency has been suggested recently by many people in the Social Service field. It is believed that such a procedure would be advantageous to both the agency and the client. Under the current system, clients often complain that their rent allowances are not for the correct amount. Agencies, in turn, have had to cope with irate landlords who complain that they are not receiving rent checks until much later than their due date.

The proposed new system would involve direct payment of the client's rent by the agency to the landlord. Clients would not receive a monthly rent allowance. Under one possible implementation of such a system, special rent payment offices would be set up in each borough and staffed by Social Service clerical personnel. Each office would handle all work involved in sending out monthly rent payments. Each client would receive monthly notification from the Social Service agency that his rent has been paid. A rent office would be established for every three Social Service centers in each borough. Only in cases where the rental exceeds $700 per month would payment be made and records kept by the Social Service center itself rather than a special rent office. However, clients would continue to make all direct contacts through the Social Service center.

Files in the rent offices would be organized on the basis of client rental. All cases involving monthly rents up to, but not exceeding, $300 would be placed in salmon-colored folders. Cases with rents from $301 to $500 would be placed in buff folders, and those with rents exceeding $500, but less than $700 would be filed in blue folders. If a client's rental changed, he would be required to notify the center as soon as possible so that this information could be brought up-to-date in his folder, and the color of his folder changed if necessary. Included in the information needed, in addition to the amount of rent, are the size of the apartment, the type of heat, and the number of flights of stairs to climb if there is no elevator.

Discussion as to whether the same information should be required of clients residing in city projects was resolved with the decision that the identical system of filing and updating of files should apply to such project tenants. The basic problem that might arise from the institution of such a program is that clients would resent being unable to pay their own rent. However, it is likely that such resentment would be only a temporary reaction to change and would disappear after the new system became standard procedure. It has been suggested that this program first be experimented with on a small scale to determine what problems may arise and how the program can be best implemented.

1. According to the passage, there are a number of complaints about the current system of rent payments. Which of the following is a *complaint* expressed in the passage? 1.____

    A. Landlords complain that clients sometimes pay the wrong amount for their rent.
    B. Landlords complain that clients sometimes do not pay their rent on time.

7

C. Clients say that the Social Service agency sometimes does not mail the rent out on time.
D. Landlords say that they sometimes fail to receive a check for the rent.

2. Assume that there are 15 Social Service centers in Manhattan. According to the passage, the number of rent offices that should be established in that borough under the new system is

   A. 1 B. 3 C. 5 D. 15

3. According to the passage, a client under the new system would receive

   A. a rent receipt from the landlord indicating that Social Services has paid the rent
   B. nothing since his rent has been paid by Social Services
   C. verification from the landlord that the rent was paid
   D. notices of rent payment from the Social Service agency

4. According to the passage, a case record involving a client whose rent has changed from $310 to $540 per month should be changed from a ____ folder to a ____ folder.

   A. blue; salmon-colored   B. buff; blue
   C. salmon-colored; blue   D. yellow; buff

5. According to the above passage, if a client's rental is lowered because of violations in his building, he would be required to notify the

   A. building department   B. landlord
   C. rent payment office   D. Social Service center

6. Which one of the following kinds of information about a rented apartment is NOT mentioned in the above passage as being necessary to include in the client's folder? The

   A. floor number, if in an apartment house with an elevator
   B. rental, if in a city project apartment
   C. size of the apartment, if in a two-family house
   D. type of heat, if in a city project apartment

7. Assume that the rent payment proposal discussed in the passage is approved and ready for implementation in the city. Which of the following actions is MOST in accordance with the proposal described in the above passage?

   A. Change over completely and quickly to the new system to avoid the confusion of having clients under both systems.
   B. Establish rent payment offices in all of the existing Social Service centers.
   C. Establish one small rent payment office in Manhattan for about six months.
   D. Set up an office in each borough and discontinue issuing rent allowances.

8. According to the passage, it can be *inferred* that the MOST important drawback of the new system would be that once a program is started, clients might feel

   A. they have less independence than they had before
   B. unable to cope with problems that mature people should be able to handle
   C. too far removed from Social Service personnel to successfully adapt to the new requirements
   D. too independent to work with the system

9. The above passage suggests that the proposed rent program be started as a pilot program rather than be instituted immediately throughout the city. Of the following possible reasons for a pilot program, the one which is stated in the passage as the MOST direct reason is that

   A. any change made would then be only on a temporary basis
   B. difficulties should be determined from small-scale implementation
   C. implementation on a wide scale is extremely difficult
   D. many clients might resent the new system

10. A report is often revised several times before final preparation and distribution in an effort to make certain the report meets the needs of the situation for which it is designed. Which of the following is the BEST way for the author to be sure that a report covers the areas he intended?

    A. Obtain a co-worker's opinion.
    B. Compare it with a content checklist.
    C. Test it on a subordinate.
    D. Check his bibliography.

11. Visual aids used in a report may be placed either in the text material or in the appendix. Deciding where to put a chart, table, or any such aid should depend on the

    A. title of the report
    B. purpose of the visual aid
    C. title of the visual aid
    D. length of the report

12. In which of the following situations is an oral report PREFERABLE to a written report? When a(n)

    A. recommendation is being made for a future plan of action
    B. department head requests immediate information
    C. long standing policy change is made
    D. analysis of complicated statistical data is involved

13. When an applicant is approved for public assistance, standard forms with certain information must be filled in.
    The GREATEST advantage of using standard forms in this situation rather than writing the report as you see fit is that

    A. the report can be acted on quickly
    B. the report can be written without directions from a supervisor
    C. needed information is less likely to be left out of the report
    D. information that is written up this way is more likely to be verified

14. In some types of reports, visual aids add interest, meaning, and support. They also provide an essential means of effectively communicating the message of the report.
    Of the following, the selection of the suitable visual aids to use with a report is LEAST dependent on the

    A. nature and scope of the report
    B. way in which the aid is to be used
    C. aids used in other reports
    D. prospective readers of the report

15. He wanted to ASCERTAIN the facts before arriving at a conclusion. The word ASCERTAIN means *most nearly*

    A. disprove B. determine C. convert D. provide

16. Did the supervisor ASSENT to her request for annual leave? The word ASSENT means *most nearly*

    A. allude B. protest C. agree D. refer

17. The new worker was fearful that the others would REBUFF her. The word REBUFF means *most nearly*

    A. ignore B. forget C. copy D. snub

18. The supervisor of that office does not CONDONE lateness. The word CONDONE means *most nearly*

    A. mind B. excuse C. punish D. remember

19. Each employee was instructed to be as CONCISE as possible when preparing a report. The word CONCISE means *most nearly*

    A. exact B. sincere C. flexible D. brief

20. Despite many requests for them, there was a SCANT supply of new blotters. The word SCANT means *most nearly*

    A. adequate
    B. abundant
    C. insufficient
    D. expensive

21. Did they REPLENISH the supply of forms in the cabinet? The word REPLENISH means *most nearly*

    A. straighten up
    B. refill
    C. sort out
    D. use

22. Employees may become bored if they are assigned DIVERSE duties. The word DIVERSE means *most nearly*

    A. interesting
    B. different
    C. challenging
    D. enjoyable

23. During the probation period, the worker proved to be INEPT. The word INEPT means *most nearly*

    A. incompetent
    B. insubordinate
    C. satisfactory
    D. uncooperative

24. The PUTATIVE father was not living with the family. The word PUTATIVE means *most nearly*

    A. reputed
    B. unemployed
    C. concerned
    D. indifferent

25. The adopted child researched various documents of VITAL STATISTICS in an effort to discover the names of his natural parents. The words VITAL STATISTICS means *most nearly* statistics relating to

    A. human life
    B. hospitals
    C. important facts
    D. health and welfare

KEY (CORRECT ANSWERS)

1. B
2. C
3. D
4. B
5. D

6. A
7. C
8. A
9. B
10. B

11. B
12. B
13. C
14. C
15. B

16. C
17. D
18. B
19. D
20. C

21. B
22. B
23. A
24. A
25. A

EXAMINATION SECTION
TEST 1

DIRECTIONS: Each question or incomplete statement is followed by several suggested answers or completions. Select the one that BEST answers the question or completes the statement. *PRINT THE LETTER OF THE CORRECT ANSWER IN THE SPACE AT THE RIGHT.*

Questions 1-4.

DIRECTIONS: Questions 1 through 4 are to be answered SOLELY on the basis of the information in the paragraphs below.

Some authorities have questioned whether the term "culture of poverty" should be used since "culture" means a design for living which is passed down from generation to generation. The culture of poverty is, however, a very useful concept if it is used with care, with recognition that poverty is a subculture, and with avoidance of the "cookie-cutter" approach. With regard to the individual, the cookie-cutter view assumes that all individuals in a culture turn out exactly alike, as if they were so many cookies. It overlooks the fact that, at least in our urban society, every individual is a member of more than one subculture; and which subculture most strongly influences his response in a given situation depends on the interaction of a great many factors, including his individual makeup and history, the specifics of the various subcultures to which he belongs, and the specifics of the given situation. It is always important to avoid the cookie-cutter view of culture, with regard to the individual and to the culture or subculture involved.

With regard to the culture as a whole, the cookie-cutter concept again assumes homogeneity and consistency. It forgets that within any one culture or subculture there are conflicts and contradictions, and that at any given moment an individual may have to choose, consciously, between conflicting values or patterns. Also, most individuals, in varying degrees, have a dual set of values - those by which they live and those they cherish as best. This point has been made and documented repeatedly about the culture of poverty.

1. The *cookie-cutter* approach assumes that

    A. members of the same *culture* are all alike
    B. *culture* stays the same from generation to generation
    C. the term *culture* should not be applied to groups who are poor
    D. there are value conflicts within most cultures

2. According to the passage, every person in our cities

    A. is involved in the conflicts of urban culture
    B. recognizes that poverty is a subculture
    C. lives by those values to which he is exposed
    D. belongs to more than one subculture

3. The above passage emphasizes that a culture is likely to contain within it

    A. one dominant set of values
    B. a number of contradictions

1.____

2.____

3.____

C. one subculture to which everyone belongs
D. members who are exactly alike

4. According to the above passage, individuals are sometimes forced to choose between

   A. cultures
   B. subcultures
   C. different sets of values
   D. a new culture and an old culture

Questions 5-8.

DIRECTIONS: Questions 5 through 8 are to be answered SOLELY on the basis of the following passage.

There are approximately 33 million poor people in the United States; 14.3 million of them are children, 5.3 million are old people, and the remainder are in other categories. Altogether, 6.5 million families live in poverty because the heads of the households cannot works they are either too old or too sick or too severely handicapped, or they are widowed or deserted mothers of young children. There are the working poor, the low-paid workers, the workers in seasonal industries, and soldiers with no additional income who are heads of families. There are the underemployed: those who would like full-time jobs but cannot find them, those employees who would like year-round work but lack the opportunity, and those who are employed below their level of training. There are the non-working poor: the older men and women With small retirement incomes and those with no income, the disabled, the physically and mentally handicapped, and the chronically sick.

5. According to the above passage, APPROXIMATELY what percent of the poor people in the United States are children?

   A. 33   B. 16   C. 20   D. 44

6. According to the above passage, people who work in seasonal industries are LIKELY to be classified as

   A. working poor   B. underemployed
   C. non-working poor   D. low-paid workers

7. According to the above passage, the category of non-working poor includes people who

   A. receive unemployment insurance
   B. cannot find full-time work
   C. are disabled or mentally handicapped
   D. are soldiers with wives and children

8. According to the above passage, among the underemployed are those who

   A. can find only part-time work
   B. are looking for their first jobs
   C. are inadequately trained
   D. depend on insufficient retirement incomes

Questions 9-18.

DIRECTIONS: Questions 9 through 18 are to be answered SOLELY on the basis of the information given in the following charts.

CHILD CARE SERVICES 1997-2001

CHILDREN IN FOSTER HOMES AND VOLUNTARY INSTITUTIONS, BY TYPE OF CARE, IN NEW YORK CITY AND UPSTATE* NEW YORK

| Year End | FOSTER FAMILY HOMES | | | Total in Foster Family Homes | Total in Voluntary Institutions | Total in Other | Total Number of Children |
	Boarding Homes	Adoptive or Free Homes	Wage, Work or Self-Supporting				
New York City							
1997	12,389	1,773	33	14,195	7,187	1,128	22,510
1998	13,271	1,953	42	15,266	7,227	1,237	23,730
1999	14,012	2,134	32	16,178	7,087	1,372	24,637
2000	14,558	2,137	29	16,724	6,717	1,437	24,778
2001	14,759	2,241	37	17,037	6,777	1,455	25,264
Upstate							
1997	14,801	2,902	90	17,793	3,012	241	21,046
1998	15,227	2,943	175	18,345	3,067	291	21,703
1999	16,042	3,261	64	19,367	2,940	273	22,580
2000	16,166	3,445	60	19,671	2,986	362	23,121
2001	16,357	3,606	55	20,018	3.024	485	23,527

*Upstate is defined as all of New York State, excluding New York City.

NUMBER OF CHILDREN, BY AGE, UNDER FOSTER FAMILY CARE IN NEW YORK CITY IN 2001

| Borough | Children's Ages | | | | | Total All Ages |
	One Year or Younger	Two Years	Three Years	Four Years	Over Four Years	
Manhattan	1,054	1,170	1,060	1,325	445	5,070
Bronx	842	1,196	1,156	1,220	484	4,882
Brooklyn	707	935	470	970	361	?
Queens	460	555	305	793	305	2,418
Richmond	270	505	160	173	112	1.224
Total All Boroughs	3,337	4,361	3,151	4,481	?	17,037

9. According to the table, Child Care Services, 1997-2001, the number of children in New York City boarding homes was AT LEAST twice the number of children in New York City voluntary institutions in _____ of the five years.

    A. *only* one   B. *only* two   C. *only* three   D. all

9._____

10. If the number of children cared for in voluntary institutions in New York State increases from 2001 to 2002 by exactly the same number as from 2000 to 2001, then the 2002 year-end total of children in voluntary institutions in New York State will be

    A. 3,062 B. 6,837 C. 7,494 D. 9,899

11. If the total number of children under child care services in New York City in 1997 was 25% more than in 1996, then the 1996 New York City total was MOST NEARLY

    A. 11,356 B. 11,647 C. 16,883 D. 18,008

12. From 1997 through 2001, the New York State five-year average of children in Child Care Services classified as *other* is MOST NEARLY

    A. 330 B. 728 C. 1,326 D. 1,656

13. Of all the children under foster family care in the Bronx in 2001, the percentage who were one year of age or younger is MOST NEARLY

    A. 16% B. 17% C. 18% D. 19%

14. Suppose that in New York State the *wage, work, or self-supporting* type of foster family care is given only to children between the ages of 14 and 18, and that, of the children in *adoptive or free home* foster care in each of the five years listed, only one percent each year are between the ages of 14 and 18.
    The TOTAL number of 14 to 18-year-olds under foster family care in Upstate New York exceeded 95 in _____ of the five years.

    A. each B. four C. three D. two

15. The average number of two-year-olds under foster family care in New York City's boroughs in 2001 is MOST NEARLY

    A. 872 B. 874 C. 875 D. 882

16. The difference between the total number of children of all ages under foster family care in Brooklyn in 2001 and the total number under foster care in Richmond that year is

    A. 1,224 B. 2,219 C. 3,443 D. 4,667

17. Suppose that by the end of 2002 the number of children one year or younger under foster family care in Queens will be twice the 2001 total, while the number of two-year-olds will be four-fifths the 2001 total.
    The 2002 total of children two years or younger under foster family care in Queens will be

    A. 2,418 B. 1,624 C. 1,364 D. 1,015

18. The TOTAL number of children over four years of age under foster care in New York City in 2001 was

    A. 1,607 B. 1,697 C. 1,707 D. 1,797

19. At the start of a year, a family was receiving a public assistance grant of $191 twice a month, on the 1st and 15th of each month. On March 1, their rent allowance was decreased from $75 to $71 a month since they had moved to a smaller apartment. On August 1, their semimonthly food allowance, which had been $40.20, was raised by 10%. In that year, the TOTAL amount of money disbursed to this family was

    A. $2,272.10
    B. $3,290.70
    C. $4,544.20
    D. $4,584.20

    19._____

20. It is discovered that a client has received double public assistance for 2 months by having been enrolled at two service centers of the Department of Social Services. The client should have received $84.00 twice a month instead of the double amount. He now agrees to repay the money by equal deductions from his public assistance check over a period of 12 months.
    What will the amount of his NEXT check be?

    A. $56   B. $70   C. $77   D. $80

    20._____

21. Suppose a study is being made of the composition of 3,550 families receiving public assistance. Of the first 1,050 families reviewed, 18% had four or more children.
    If, in the remaining number of families, the percentage with four or more children is half as high as the percentage in the group already reviewed, then the percentage of families with four or more children in the entire group of families is MOST NEARLY

    A. 12   B. 14   C. 16   D. 27

    21._____

22. Suppose that food prices have risen 13%, and an increase of the same amount has been granted in the food allotment given to people receiving public assistance.
    If a family has been receiving $405 a month, 35% of which is allotted for food, then the TOTAL amount of public assistance this family receives per month will be changed to

    A. $402.71   B. $420.03   C. $423.43   D. $449.71

    22._____

23. Assume that the food allowance is to be raised 5% in August but will be retroactive for four months to April. The retroactive allowance is to be divided into equal sections and added to the public assistance checks for August, September, October, November, and December.
    A family which has been receiving $420 monthly, 40% of which was allotted for food, will receive what size check in August?

    A. $426.72   B. $428.40   C. $430.50   D. $435.12

    23._____

24. A blind client, who receives $105 public assistance twice a month, inherits 14 shares of stock worth $90 each. The client is required to sell the stock and spend his inheritance before receiving more public assistance.
    Using his public assistance allowance as a guide, how many months are his new assets expected to last?

    A. 6   B. 7   C. 8   D. 12

    24._____

25. The Department of Social Services has 16 service centers in Manhattan. These centers may be divided into those which are downtown (south of Central Park) and those which are uptown. Two of the centers are special service centers and are downtown, while the remainder of the centers are general service centers. There is a total of 7 service centers downtown.
The percentage of the general service centers which are uptown is MOST NEARLY

   A. 56   B. 64   C. 69   D. 79

KEY (CORRECT ANSWERS)

1. A
2. D
3. B
4. C
5. D

6. A
7. C
8. A
9. B
10. D

11. D
12. D
13. B
14. C
15. A

16. B
17. C
18. C
19. D
20. B

21. A
22. C
23. D
24. A
25. B

TEST 2

DIRECTIONS: Each question or incomplete statement is followed by several suggested answers or completions. Select the one that BEST answers the question or completes the statement. *PRINT THE LETTER OF THE CORRECT ANSWER IN THE SPACE AT THE RIGHT.*

1. On January 1, a family was receiving supplementary monthly public assistance of $56 for food, $48 for rent, and $28 for other necessities. In the spring, their rent rose by 10%, and their rent allowance was adjusted accordingly.
   In the summer, due to the death of a family member, their allotments for food and other necessities were reduced by 1/7.
   Their monthly allowance check in the fall should be

   A. $124.80　　B. $128.80　　C. $132.80　　D. $136.80

   1.____

2. Twice a month, a certain family receives a $170 general allowance for rent, food, and clothing expenses. In addition, the family receives a specific supplementary allotment for utilities of $192 a year, which is added to their semi-monthly check.
   If the general allowance alone is reduced by 5%, what will be the TOTAL amount of their next semi-monthly check?

   A. $161.50　　B. $169.50　　C. $170.00　　D. $177.50

   2.____

3. If each clerk in a certain unit sees an average of 9 clients in a 7-hour day and there are 15 clerks in the unit, APPROXIMATELY how many clients will be seen in a 35-hour week?

   A. 315　　B. 405　　C. 675　　D. 945

   3.____

4. The program providing federal welfare aid to the state and its cities is intended to expand services to public assistance recipients.
   All of the following services are included in the program EXCEPT

   A. homemaker/housekeeper services
   B. mental health clinics
   C. abortion clinics
   D. narcotic addiction control services

   4.____

5. The Department of Consumer Affairs is NOT concerned with regulation of

   A. prices　　　　　　　　B. product service guarantees
   C. welfare fraud　　　　D. product misrepresentation

   5.____

6. A plan to control the loss of welfare monies would likely contain all of the following EXCEPT

   A. identification cards with photographs of the welfare client
   B. individual cash payments to each member of a family
   C. computerized processing of welfare money records
   D. face-to-face interviews with the welfare clients

   6.____

7. The state law currently allows a woman to obtain an abortion 7.____

   A. only if it is intended to save her life
   B. if three doctors confirm the need for such treatment
   C. if it does not conflict with her religious beliefs
   D. upon her request, up to the 24th week of pregnancy

8. Under the city's public assistance program, allocations for payment of a client's rent and 8.____
   security deposits are given in check form directly to the welfare recipient and not to the
   landlord.
   This practice is used in the city MAINLY as an effort to

   A. increase the client's responsibility for his own affairs
   B. curb the rent overcharges made by most landlords in the city
   C. control the number of welfare recipients housed in public housing projects
   D. limit the number of checks issued to each welfare family

9. The city plans to save 100 million dollars a year in public assistance costs. 9.____
   To achieve this goal, the Human Resources Administration and the Department of
   Social Services may take any of the following steps EXCEPT

   A. tightening controls on public assistance eligibility requirements
   B. intensifying the investigations of relief frauds
   C. freezing the salaries of all agency employees for a one-year period
   D. cutting the services extended to public assistance clients

10. Recently, the state instituted a work relief program under which employable recipients of 10.____
    Home Relief and Aid to Dependent Children are given jobs to help work off their relief
    grants.
    Under the present work relief program, program recipients are NOT required to

    A. report to state employment offices every two weeks to pick up their welfare checks
    B. live within a two-mile radius of the job site to which they are referred
    C. respond to offers of part-time jobs in public agencies
    D. take job training courses offered through the State Employment Service

11. Of the following, the MOST inclusive program designed to help selected cities to sub- 11.____
    stantially improve social, physical, and economic conditions in specially selected slum
    neighborhoods is known as the

    A. Model Cities Program
    B. Neighborhood Youth Corps Program
    C. Urban Renewal Program
    D. Emergency Employment Act

12. The crusade against environmental hazards in the United States is concentrated in 12.____
    urban areas MOSTLY on the problems of

    A. air pollution, sewage treatment, and noise
    B. garbage collection
    C. automobile exhaust fumes and street cleanliness
    D. recycling, reconstitution, and open space

Questions 13-16.

DIRECTIONS: Questions 13 through 16 are to be answered SOLELY on the basis of the information in the following passage.

City social work agencies and the police have been meeting at City Hall to coordinate efforts to defuse the tensions among teenage groups that they fear could flare into warfare once summer vacations begin. Police intelligence units, with the help of the District Attorneys' offices, are gathering information to identify gangs and their territories. A list of 3,000 gang members has already been assembled, and 110 gangs have been identified. Social workers from various agencies like the Department of Social Services, Neighborhood youth Corps, and the Youth Board are out every day developing liaison with groups of juveniles through meetings at schools and recreation centers. Many street workers spend their days seeking to ease the intergang hostility, tracing potentially incendiary rumors, and trying to channel willing gang members into participation in established summer programs. The city's Youth Services Agency plans to spend a million dollars for special summer programs in ten main city areas where gang activity is most firmly entrenched. Five of the "gang neighborhoods" are clustered in an area forming most of southeastern Bronx, and it is here that most of the 110 identified gangs have formed. Special Youth Services programs will also be directed toward the Rockaway section of Queens, Chinatown, Washington Heights, and two neighborhoods in northern Staten Island noted for a lot of motorcycle gang activity. Some of these programs will emphasize sports and recreation, others vocational guidance or neighborhood improvement, but each program will be aimed at benefiting all youngsters in the area. Although none of the money will be spent specifically on gang members, the Youth Services Agency is consulting gang leaders, along with other teenagers, on the projects they would like developed in their area.

13. The above passage states that one of the steps taken by street workers in trying to defuse the tensions among teenage gangs is that of

    A. conducting summer school sessions that will benefit all neighborhood youth
    B. monitoring neighborhood sports competitions between rival gangs
    C. developing liaison with community school boards and parent associations
    D. tracing rumors that could intensify intergang hostilities

14. Based on the information given in the above passage on gangs and New York City's gang members, it is CORRECT to state that

    A. there are no teenage gangs located in Brooklyn
    B. most of the gangs identified by the police are concentrated in one borough
    C. there is a total of 110 gangs in New York City
    D. only a small percentage of gangs in New York City is in Queens

15. According to the above passage, one IMPORTANT aspect of the program is that

    A. youth gang leaders and other teenagers are involved in the planning
    B. money will be given directly to gang members for use on their projects
    C. only gang members will be allowed to participate in the programs
    D. the parents of gang members will act as youth leaders

16. Various city agencies are cooperating in the attempt to keep the city's youth *cool* during the summer school vacation period.
The above passage does NOT specifically indicate participation in this project by the

    A. Police Department
    B. District Attorney's Office
    C. Board of Education
    D. Department of Social Services

Questions 17-19.

DIRECTIONS: Questions 17 through 19 are to be answered SOLELY on the basis of the information in the following passage.

It is important that interviewers understand to some degree the manner in which stereotyped thinking operates. Stereotypes are commonly held, but predominantly false, preconceptions about the appearance and traits of individuals of different racial, religious, ethnic, and subcultural groups. Distinct traits, physical and mental, are associated with each group, and membership in a particular group is enough, in the mind of a person holding the stereotype, to assure that these traits will be perceived in individuals who are members of that group. Conversely, possession of the particular stereotyped trait by an individual usually indicates to the holder of the stereotype that the individual is a group member. Linked to the formation of stereotypes is the fact that mental traits, either positive or negative, such as honesty, laziness, avariciousness, and other characteristics are associated with particular stereotypes. Either kind of stereotype, if held by an interviewer, can seriously damage the results of an interview. In general, stereotypes can be particularly dangerous when they are part of the belief patterns of administrators, interviewers, and supervisors, who are in a position to affect the lives of others and to stimulate or retard the development of human potential. The holding of a stereotype by an interviewer, for example, diverts his attention from significant essential facts and information upon which really valid assessments may be made. Unfortunately, it is the rare interviewer who is completely conscious of the real basis upon which he is making his evaluation of the people he is interviewing. The specific reasons given by an interviewer for a negative evaluation, even though apparently logical and based upon what, in the mind of the interviewer, are very good reasons, may not be the truly motivating factors. This is why the careful selection and training of interviewers is such an important responsibility of an agency which is attempting to help a great diversity of human beings.

17. Of the following, the BEST title for the above paragraph is

    A. POSITIVE AND NEGATIVE EFFECTS OF STEREOTYPED THINKING
    B. THE RELATIONSHIP OF STEREOTYPES TO INTERVIEWING
    C. AN AGENCY'S RESPONSIBILITY IN INTERVIEWING
    D. THE IMPACT OF STEREOTYPED THINKING ON PROFESSIONAL FUNCTIONS

18. According to the above passage, MOST interviewers

    A. compensate for stereotyped beliefs to avoid negatively affecting the results of their interviews
    B. are influenced by stereotypes they hold, but put greater stress on factual information developed during the interview
    C. are seldom aware of their real motives when evaluating interviewees
    D. give logical and good reasons for negative evaluations of interviewees

19. According to the above passage, which of the following is NOT a characteristic of stereo- 19.____
    types?

    A. Stereotypes influence estimates of personality traits of people.
    B. Positive stereotypes can damage the results of an interview.
    C. Physical traits associated with stereotypes seldom really exist.
    D. Stereotypes sometimes are a basis upon which valid personality assessments can be made.

Questions 20-25.

DIRECTIONS: Questions 20 through 25 are to be answered SOLELY on the basis of the information in the following passage.

The quality of the voice of a worker is an important factor in conveying to clients and co-workers his attitude and, to some degree, his character. The human voice, when not consciously disguised, may reflect a person's mood, temper, and personality. It has been shown in several experiments that certain character traits can be assessed with better than chance accuracy through listening to the voice of an unknown person who cannot be seen.

Since one of the objectives of the worker is to put clients at ease and to present an encouraging and comfortable atmosphere, a harsh, shrill, or loud voice could have a negative effect. A client who displays emotions of anger or resentment would probably be provoked even further by a caustic tone. In a face-to-face situation, an unpleasant voice may be compensated for to some degree by a concerned and kind facial expression. However, when one speaks on the telephone, the expression on one's face cannot be seen by the listener. A supervising clerk who wishes to represent himself effectively to clients should try to eliminate as many faults as possible in striving to develop desirable voice qualities.

20. If a worker uses a sarcastic tone while interviewing a resentful client, the client, accord- 20.____
    ing to the above passage, would MOST likely

    A. avoid the face-to-face situation
    B. be ashamed of his behavior
    C. become more resentful
    D. be provoked to violence

21. According to the above passage, experiments comparing voice and character traits have 21.____
    demonstrated that

    A. prospects for improving an unpleasant voice through training are better than chance
    B. the voice can be altered to project many different psychological characteristics
    C. the quality of the human voice reveals more about the speaker than his words do
    D. the speaker's voice tells the hearer something about the speaker's personality

22. Which of the following, according to the above passage, is a person's voice MOST likely 22.____
    to reveal?
    His

    A. prejudices   B. intelligence
    C. social awareness   D. temperament

23. It may be MOST reasonably concluded from the above passage that an interested and sympathetic expression on the face of a worker

    A. may induce a client to feel certain he will receive welfare benefits
    B. will eliminate the need for pleasant vocal qualities in the interviewer
    C. may help to make up for an unpleasant voice in the interviewer
    D. is desirable as the interviewer speaks on the telephone to a client

24. Of the following, the MOST reasonable implication of the above paragraph is that a worker should, when speaking to a client, control and use his voice to

    A. simulate a feeling of interest in the problems of the client
    B. express his emotions directly and adequately
    C. help produce in the client a sense of comfort and security
    D. reflect his own true personality

25. It may be concluded from the passage that the PARTICULAR reason for a worker to pay special attention to modulating her voice when talking on the phone to a client is that, during a telephone conversation,

    A. there is a necessity to compensate for the way in which a telephone distorts the voice
    B. the voice of the worker is a reflection of her mood and character
    C. the client can react only on the basis of the voice and words she hears
    D. the client may have difficulty getting a clear understanding over the telephone

KEY (CORRECT ANSWERS)

1.	A	11.	A
2.	B	12.	A
3.	C	13.	D
4.	C	14.	B
5.	C	15.	A
6.	B	16.	C
7.	D	17.	B
8.	A	18.	C
9.	C	19.	D
10.	B	20.	C

21. D
22. D
23. C
24. C
25. C

EXAMINATION SECTION
TEST 1

DIRECTIONS: Each question or incomplete statement is followed by several suggested answers or completions. Select the one that BEST answers the question or completes the statement. *PRINT THE LETTER OF THE CORRECT ANSWER IN THE SPACE AT THE RIGHT.*

1. Assume that an applicant, obviously under a great deal of stress, talks continuously and rambles, making it difficult for you to determine the exact problem and her need. In order to make the interview more successful, it would be BEST for you to
    A. interrupt the applicant and ask her specific questions in order to get the information you need
    B. tell the applicant that her rambling may be a basic cause of her problem
    C. let the applicant continue talking as long as she wishes
    D. ask the applicant to get to the point because other people are waiting for you

1.____

2. A worker must be able to interview clients all day and still be able to listen and maintain interest.
Of the following, it is MOST important for you to show interest in the client because, if you appear interested,
    A. the client is more likely to appreciate your professional status
    B. the client is more likely to disclose a greater amount of information
    C. the client is less likely to tell lies
    D. you are more likely to gain your supervisor's approval

2.____

3. The application process is overwhelming to applicant Ms. M. She is very anxious and is fearful that she does not have all that she needs to be eligible for assistance. As a result, every time she is asked to produce a verifying document during the interview, she fumbles and drops all the other documents to the floor.
Of the following, the MOST effective method for you to use to complete the application process is to
    A. ask Ms. M not to be so nervous because you cannot get the work done if she fusses so much
    B. take the documents away from Ms. M and do it your self
    C. suggest that Ms. M get a friend to come and help her with the papers
    D. try to calm Ms. M and tell her that you are willing to help her with the papers to get the information you require

3.____

4. An applicant for public assistance claims that her husband deserted the family and that she needs money immediately for food since her children have not eaten for two days. Under normal procedure, she has to wait several days before she can be given any money for this purpose. In accordance with departmental policy, no exception can be made in this case.
Of the following, the BEST action for you to take is to
   A. tell her that, according to departmental policy, she cannot be given money immediately
   B. purchase some food for her, using your own funds, so that she can feed her children
   C. take up a collection among co-workers
   D. send her to another center

5. Applicants for public assistance often complain about the length of the application form. They also claim that the questions are too personal, since all they want is money. It is true that the form is long, but the answers to all the questions on the form are needed so that the department can make a decision on eligibility.
When applicants complain, which of the following would be the MOST appropriate action for you to take?
   A. Help such applicants understand that each question has a purpose which will help in the determination of eligibility
   B. Tell such applicants that you agree but that you must comply with regulations because it is your job
   C. Tell such applicants that they should stop complaining if they want you to help
   D. Refer such applicants to a supervisor who will explain agency policy

6. Which one of the following statements BEST describes the primary goal of a worker?
   A. Process as many clients in as short a time as possible
   B. Help his clients
   C. Grow into a more understanding person
   D. Assert his authority

7. Restating a question before the person being interviewed gives an answer to the original question is usually NOT good practice *principally* because
   A. the client will think that you don't know your job
   B. it may confuse the client
   C. the interviewer should know exactly what to ask and how to put the question
   D. it reveals the interviewer's insecurity

8. A white worker can BEST improve his ability to work with black clients if he
   A. tries to forget that the clients are black
   B. tells the black clients that he has no prejudices
   C. becomes aware of the problems black clients face
   D. socializes with black workers in the agency

9. A client warns that if he does not get what he wants he will report you to your supervisor and, if necessary, to the mayor's office.
   Of the following, the MOST appropriate response for you to make in this situation is to
   A. encourage the client to do as he threatens because you know that you are right
   B. call your supervisor in so that the client may confront him
   C. explain to the client how the decision will be made on his request and suggest what action he can take if there is an adverse decision
   D. try to understand the client's problem but tell him that he must not explode in the office because you will have to ask him to leave if he does

9._____

Questions 10-20.

DIRECTIONS: Refer to the following Semi-Monthly Family Allowance Schedule and Conversion Table when answering Questions 10 through 20.

SEMI-MONTHLY FAMILY ALLOWANCE SCHEDULE
(Based on Number of Persons in Household)

NUMBER OF PERSONS IN HOUSEHOLD						
One	Two	Three	Four	Five	Six	Each Additional Person
$470.00	$750.00	$1000.00	$1290.00	$1590.00	$1840.00	$25.00

CONVERSION TABLE - WEEKLY TO SEMI-MONTHLY AMOUNTS

DOLLARS				CENTS			
Weekly Amount	Semi-Monthly Amount	Weekly Amount	Semi-Monthly Amount	Weekly Amount	Semi-Monthly Amount	Weekly Amount	Semi-Monthly Amount
$10.00	$21.70	$510.00	$1105.00	$0.10	$0.20	$5.10	$11.10
20.00	43.30	520.00	1126.70	0.20	0.40	5.20	11.30
30.00	65.00	530.00	1148.30	0.30	0.70	5.30	11.50
40.00	86.70	540.00	1170.00	0.40	0.90	5.40	11.70
50.00	108.30	550.00	1191.70	0.50	1.10	5.50	11.90
60.00	130.00	560.00	1213.30	0.60	1.30	5.60	12.10
70.00	151.70	570.00	1235.00	0.70	1.50	5.70	12.40
80.00	173.30	580.00	1256.70	0.80	1.70	5.80	12.60
90.00	195.00	590.00	1278.30	0.90	2.00	5.90	12.80
100.00	216.70	600.00	1300.00	1.00	2.20	6.00	13.00
110.00	238.30	610.00	1321.70	1.10	2.40	6.10	13.20
120.00	260.00	620.00	1343.30	1.20	2.60	6.20	13.40
130.00	281.70	630.00	1365.00	1.30	2.80	6.30	13.70
140.00	303.30	640.00	1386.70	1.40	3.00	6.40	13.90
150.00	325.00	650.00	1408.30	1.50	3.30	6.50	14.10
160.00	346.70	660.00	1430.00	1.60	3.50	6.60	14.30
170.00	368.30	670.00	1451.70	1.70	3.70	6.70	14.50
180.00	390.00	680.00	1473.30	1.80	3.90	6.80	14.70
190.00	411.70	690.00	1495.00	1.90	4.10	6.90	15.00
200.00	433.30	700.00	1516.70	2.00	4.30	7.00	15.20
210.00	455.00	710.00	1538.30	2.10	4.60	7.10	15.40
220.00	476.70	720.00	1560.00	2.20	4.80	7.20	15.60
230.00	498.30	730.00	1581.70	2.30	5.00	7.30	15.80
240.00	520.00	740.00	1603.30	2.40	5.20	7.40	16.00
250.00	541.70	750.00	1625.00	2.50	5.40	7.50	16.30
260.00	563.30	760.00	1646.70	2.60	5.60	7.60	16.50
270.00	585.00	770.00	1668.30	2.70	5.90	7.70	16.70
280.00	606.70	780.00	1690.00	2.80	6.10	7.80	16.90
290.00	628.30	790.00	1711.70	2.90	6.30	7.90	17.10
300.00	650.00	800.00	1733.30	3.00	6.50	8.00	17.30
310.00	671.70	810.00	1755.00	3.10	6.70	8.10	17.60
320.00	693.30	820.00	1776.70	3.20	6.90	8.20	17.80
330.00	715.00	830.00	1798.30	3.30	7.20	8.30	18.00
340.00	736.70	840.00	1820.00	3.40	7.40	8.40	18.20
350.00	783.00	850.00	1841.70	3.50	7.60	8.50	18.40
360.00	780.00	860.00	1863.30	3.60	7.80	8.60	18.60
370.00	801.70	870.00	1885.00	3.70	8.00	8.70	18.90
380.00	823.30	880.00	1906.70	3.80	8.20	8.80	19.10
390.00	845.00	890.00	1928.30	3.90	8.50	8.90	18.30
400.00	866.70	900.00	1950.00	4.00	8.70	9.00	19.50
410.00	888.30	910.00	1971.70	4.10	8.90	9.10	19.70
420.00	910.00	920.00	1993.30	4.20	9.10	9.20	19.90
430.00	931.70	930.00	2015.00	4.30	9.30	9.30	20.20
440.00	953.30	940.00	2036.70	4.40	9.50	9.40	20.40
450.00	975.00	950.00	2058.30	4.50	9.80	9.50	20.60
460.00	996.70	960.00	2080.00	4.60	10.00	9.60	20.80
470.00	1018.30	970.00	2101.70	4.70	10.20	9.70	21.00
480.00	1040.00	980.00	2123.30	4.80	10.40	9.80	21.20
490.00	1061.70	990.00	2145.00	4.90	10.60	9.90	21.50
500.00	1083.30	1000.00	2166.70	5.00	10.80		

NOTE: Questions 10 through 20 are to be answered SOLELY on the basis of the Schedule and Table given above and the information and case situations given below.

Questions 10 through 14 are based on Case Situation #1.
Questions 15 through 20 are based on Case Situation #2.

Public assistance grants are computed on a semi-monthly basis. This means that all figures are first broken down into semi-monthly amounts, and that when a client receives a check twice a month, each semi-monthly check covers his requirements for a period of approximately 2-1/6 weeks. The grants are computed by means of the following procedures.

1. Determine the semi-monthly allowance for the family from the Semi-Monthly Family Allowance Schedule.
2. Determine total semi-monthly income by deducting from the semi-monthly gross earnings (the wages or salary *before* payroll deductions) all semi-monthly expenses for federal, state, and city income taxes, Social Security payments, State Disability Insurance payments, union dues, cost of transportation, and $10.00 per work day for lunch.
3. Add the semi-monthly allowance and the semi-monthly rent (monthly rent must be divided in half).
4. Subtract the semi-monthly income (if there is any income).
5. The formula for computing the semi-monthly grant is:
   Family Allowance + Rent (semi-monthly)
   Total Income (semi-monthly)
   = Amount of Grant (semi-monthly)
6. Refer to the Conversion Table in order to convert weekly amounts into semi-monthly amounts.

CASE SITUATION #1

The Smiths receive public assistance. The family includes John Smith, his wife Barbara, and their four children. They occupy a five-room apartment for which the rent is $1050.00 per month. Mr. Smith is employed as a cleaner and his gross wages are $1000 per week. He is employed 5 days a week and spends $7.00 a day carfare. He buys his lunches. The following weekly deductions are made from his salary:

Social Security	$60.00
Disability Benefits	3.80
Federal Income Tax	43.00
State Income Tax	28.00
City Income Tax	10.00

CASE SITUATION #2

The Jones family receives public assistance. The family includes Steven and Diane Jones and their two children. They occupy a four-room apartment for which the rental is $850.00 a month. Mr. Jones is employed as a handyman, and his gross wages are $900 per week. He is employed 4 days a week and spends $7.00 a day carfare. He buys his lunches. He has the following weekly deductions made from his salary:

Social Security	$40.00
Disability Benefits	2.70
Federal Income Tax	38.90
State Income Tax	20.50
City Income Tax	6.20

10. The weekly amount that Mr. Smith contributes towards Social Security, Disability Benefits, and income taxes is
    A. $313.70   B. $231.40   C. $144.80   D. $106.80

11. The semi-monthly family allowance for the Smith family is
    A. $1290.00   B. $1590.00   C. $1840.00   D. $1845.00

12. What is the total of semi-monthly expenses related to Mr. Smith's employment which will be deducted from semi-monthly gross earnings to compute semi-monthly income?
    A. $497.80   B. $422.00   C. $389.50   D. $229.80

13. Which of the following amounts is the total semi-monthly income for the Smith family?
    A. $2166.70   B. $2000.00   C. $1668.90   D. $1004.40

14. The amount of the grant which the Smith family is entitled to receive is
    A. $2365.00   B. $1840.00   C. $1392.20   D. $696.10

15. The weekly amount that Mr. Jones contributes towards Social Security, Disability Benefits, and income taxes is
    A. $108.30   B. $176.30   C. $234.30   D. $234.70

16. The semi-monthly family allowance for the Jones family is
    A. $750.00   B. $1000.00   C. $1220.00   D. $1290.00

17. The total of semi-monthly expenses related to Mr. Jones' employment which will be deducted from semi-monthly gross earnings is
    A. $172.30   B. $189.30   C. $382.00   D. $407.20

18. Which of the following amounts is the total semi-monthly income for the Jones family? 18._____
    A. $1282.00	B. $1553.20	C. $1568.00	D. $2122.30

19. The grant which the Jones family will receive is 19._____
    A. $147.00	B. $294.00	C. $1290.00	D. $1715.00

20. If Mrs. Jones' monthly rent had been $1050, what would the amount of the grant be? 20._____
    A. $247.00	B. $494.00	C. $772.00	D. $1822.00

KEY (CORRECT ANSWERS)

1.	A	11.	C
2.	B	12.	A
3.	D	13.	C
4.	A	14.	D
5.	A	15.	A
6.	B	16.	D
7.	B	17.	C
8.	C	18.	C
9.	C	19.	A
10.	C	20.	A

TEST 2

DIRECTIONS: Each question or incomplete statement is followed by several suggested answers or completions. Select the one that BEST answers the question or completes the statement. *PRINT THE LETTER OF THE CORRECT ANSWER IN THE SPACE AT THE RIGHT.*

Questions 1-5.

DIRECTIONS: Each of Questions 1 through 5 consists of information given in outline form and four sentences labeled A, B, C, and D. For each question, choose the one sentence which CORRECTLY expresses the information given in outline form and which also displays PROPER English usage.

1. Client's Name - Joanna Jones
    Number of Children - 3
    Client's Income - None
    Client's Marital Status - Single
    - A. Joanna Jones is an unmarried client with three children who have no income.
    - B. Joanna Jones, who is single and has no income, a client she has three children.
    - C. Joanna Jones, whose three children are clients, is single and has no income.
    - D. Joanna Jones, who has three children, is an unmarried client with no income.

1.___

2. Client's Name - Bertha Smith
    Number of Children - 2
    Client's Rent - $1050 per month
    Number of Rooms- 4
    - A. Bertha Smith, a client, pays $1050 per month for her four rooms with two children.
    - B. Client Bertha Smith has two children and pays $1050 per month for four rooms.
    - C. Client Bertha Smith is paying $1050 per month for two children with four rooms.
    - D. For four rooms and two children, Client Bertha Smith pays $1050 per month.

2.___

3. Name of Employee - Cynthia Dawes
    Number of Cases Assigned - 9
    Date Cases Were Assigned - 12/16
    Number of Assigned Cases Completed - 8
    - A. On December 16, employee Cynthia Dawes was assigned nine cases; she has completed eight of these cases.
    - B. Cynthia Dawes, employee on December 16, assigned nine cases, completed eight.
    - C. Being employed on December 16, Cynthia Dawes completed eight of nine assigned cases.
    - D. Employee Cynthia Dawes, she was assigned nine cases and completed eight, on December 16.

3.___

4. Place of Audit - Broadway Center
    Names of Auditors - Paul Cahn, Raymond Perez
    Date of Audit - 11/20
    Number of Cases Audited - 41
    - A. On November 20, at the Broadway Center 41 cases was audited by auditors Paul Cahn and Raymond Perez.
    - B. Auditors Raymond Perez and Paul Cahn has audited 41 cases at the Broadway

4.___

       Center, on November 20.
- C. At the Broadway Center, on November 20, auditors Paul Cahn and Raymond Perez audited 41 cases.
- D. Auditors Paul Cahn and Raymond Perez at the Broadway Center, on November 20, is auditing 41 cases.

5. Name of Client - Barbra Levine   5.____
    Client's Monthly Income - $2100
    Client's Monthly Expenses - $4520
- A. Barbra Levine is a client, her monthly income is $2100 and her monthly expenses is $4520.
- B. Barbra Levine's monthly income is $2100 and she is a client, with whose monthly expenses are $4520.
- C. Barbra Levine is a client whose monthly income is $2100 and whose monthly expenses are $4520.
- D. Barbra Levine, a client, is with a monthly income which is $2100 and monthly expenses which are $4520.

Questions 6-10.

DIRECTIONS: Questions 6 through 10 are to be answered SOLELY on the basis of the information contained in the following passage.

    Any person who is living in New York City and is otherwise eligible may be granted public assistance whether or not he has New York State residence. However, since New York City does not contribute to the cost of assistance granted to persons who are without State residence, the cases of all recipients must be formally identified as to whether or not each member of the household has State residence.

    To acquire State residence a person must have resided in New York State continuously for one year. Such residence is not lost unless the person is out of the State continuously for a period of one year or longer. Continuous residence does not include any period during which the individual is a patient in a hospital, an inmate of a public institution or of an incorporated private institution, a resident on a military reservation or a minor residing in a boarding home while under the care of an authorized agency. Receipt of public assistance does not prevent a person from acquiring State residence. State residence, once acquired, is not lost because of absence from the State while a person is serving in the U.S. Armed Forces or the Merchant Marine; nor does a member of the family of such a person lose State residence while living with or near that person in these circumstances.

    Each person, regardless of age, acquires or loses State residence as an individual. There is no derivative State residence except for an infant at the time of birth. He is deemed to have State residence if he is in the custody of both parents and either one of them has State residence, or if the parent having custody of him has State residence.

6. According to the above passage, an infant is deemed to have New York State residence at the time of his birth *if*
   A. he is born in New York State but neither of his parents is a resident
   B. he is in the custody of only one parent, who is not a resident, but his other parent is a resident
   C. his brother and sister are residents
   D. he is in the custody of both his parents but only one of them is a resident

6._____

7. The Jones family consists of five members. Jack and Mary Jones have lived in New York State continuously for the past eighteen months after having lived in Ohio since they were born. Of their three children, one was born ten months ago and has been in the custody of his parents since birth. Their second child lived in Ohio until six months ago and then moved in with his parents. Their third child had never lived in New York until he moved with his parents to New York eighteen months ago. However, he entered the armed forces one month later and has not lived in New York since that time.
   Based on the above passage, how many members of the Jones family are New York State residents?
   A. 2   B. 3   C. 4   D. 5

7._____

8. Assuming that each of the following individuals has lived continuously in New York State for the past year, and has never previously lived in the State, which one of them is a New York State resident?
   A. Jack Salinas, who has been an inmate in a State correctional facility for six months of the year
   B. Fran Johnson, who has lived on an Army base for the entire year
   C. Arlene Snyder, who married a non-resident during the past year
   D. Gary Phillips, who was a patient in a Veterans Administration hospital for the entire year

8._____

9. The above passage implies that the reason for determining whether or not a recipient of public assistance is a State resident is that
   A. the cost of assistance for non-residents is not a New York City responsibility
   B. non-residents living in New York City are not eligible for public assistance
   C. recipients of public assistance are barred from acquiring State residence
   D. New York City is responsible for the full cost of assistance to recipients who are residents

9._____

10. Assume that the Rollins household in New York City consists of six members at the present time - Anne Rollins, her three children, her aunt and her uncle. Anne Rollins and one of her children moved to New York City seven months ago. Neither of them had previously lived in New York State. Her other two children have lived in New York City continuously for the past two years, as has her aunt. Anne Rollins' uncle had lived in New York City continuously for many years until two years ago. He then entered the armed forces and has returned to New York City within the past month.
    Based on the above passage, how many members of the Rollins' household are New York State residents?
    A. 2   B. 3   C. 4   D. 6

10._____

11. You are interviewing a client to determine whether financial assistance should be continued and you find that what he is telling you does not agree exactly with your records.
    Of the following, the BEST way to handle this situation is to
    A. recommend that his public assistance payments be stopped, since you have caught him lying to you
    B. tell the client about the points of disagreement and ask him if he can clear them up
    C. give the client the benefit of the doubt and recommend continuation of his payments
    D. show the client the records and warn him that he must either tell the truth or lose his benefits

11.____

12. An applicant for public assistance gets angry at some of the questions you must ask her.
    Of the following, the BEST way to handle this situation is to
    A. assume that she is trying to hide something, and end the interview
    B. skip the questions that bother her and come back to them at the end of the interview
    C. tell her that she must either answer the question or leave
    D. explain to her that you are required to get answers to all the questions in order to be able to help her

12.____

13. At the end of an interview to determine whether financial assistance should be continued, the client offers to take you to lunch.
    Of the following, the BEST response to such an invitation is to
    A. tell the client that you do not take bribes and report the matter to your supervisor
    B. accept the invitation if you have the time, but do not let it influence your recommendation as to his eligibility for continuing public assistance
    C. politely refuse the invitation, and do not let it influence your recommendation as to his continuing eligibility for public assistance
    D. point out to the client that his budget does not include money for entertainment

13.____

Questions 14-18.

DIRECTIONS: Questions 14 through 18 are to be answered SOLELY on the basis of the information, the assumptions, and the table given below.

Each question describes an applicant family. You are to determine into which of the four categories (A, B, C, or D) each of the applicant families should be placed. In order to do this, you must match the description of the applicant family with the factors determining eligibility for each of the four categories. Each applicant family must meet ALL of the criteria for the category.

ASSUMPTIONS FOR ALL QUESTIONS
The information in the following tables does NOT necessarily reflect actual practice in the Department of Social Services.
1. The date of application is January 25.
   Each applicant family that cannot be placed in categories A, B, or C must be placed in category D.
2. A *dependent child* is a child who is less than 18 years of age, or less than 21 years of age if attending school full time, who depends upon its parents for support.
3. A mother in a family with one or more dependent children is not expected to work and her work status is not to be considered in establishing the category of the family.

5 (#2)

CATEGORY OF APPLICANT FAMILY	FACTORS DETERMINING ELIGIBILITY
A	1. There is at least one dependent child in the home. 2. Children are deprived of parental support because father is: 　(a) Deceased 　(b) Absent from the home 　(c) Incapacitated due to medically verified illness 　(d) Over age 65 　(e) Not fully employed because of verified ill health 3. Parents or guardians reside in the same home as the children. 4. Applicant family must have resided in the State for a period of one year or more.
B	1. There is at least one dependent child in the home. 2. Both parents are in the home and are not incapacitated. 3. Both parents are the children's natural parents. 4. Father unemployed or works less than 70 hours per month. 5. Father has recent work history. 6. Father not currently receiving Unemployment Insurance Benefits. 7. Father available and willing to work. 8. Applicant family must have resided in the State for a period of one year or more.
C	1. There is a war veteran in the home. 2. Applicant families do not meet the criteria for Categories A or B.
D	Applicant families do not meet the criteria for Categories A, B, or C

14. Woman, aged 52, with child 6 years old who she states was left in her home at the age of 2. Woman states child is her niece, and that she has no knowledge of whereabouts of parents or any other relatives. Both woman and child have resided in the State since June 15.   14. ___

15. Married couple with 2 dependent children at home. Family has resided in the State for the last 5 years. Wife cannot work. Husband, veteran of Gulf War, can work only 15 hours a week due to kidney ailment (verified).   15. ___

16. Married couple, both aged 35, with 3 dependent children at home, 1 of whom is 17 years of age. Wife available for work and presently working 2 days a week, 7 hours each day. Husband, who was laid off two weeks ago, is not eligible for Unemployment Insurance Benefits. Family has resided in the State since January 1, 2002.

16. ____

17. Married couple with 1 dependent child at home. They have resided in the State since January 25, 2001. Wife must remain home to take care of child. Husband veteran of Gulf War. Husband is available for work on a limited basis because of heart condition which has been verified. A second child, a married 17-year-old son, lives in California.

17. ____

18. Married couple with 2 children, ages 6 and 12, at home. Family has resided in the State since June 2, 1998. Wife not available for work. Husband, who served in the Iraqi War, was laid off 3 weeks ago and is receiving Unemployment Insurance Benefits of $500.00 weekly.

18. ____

19. Of the following, the MOST important reason for referring a public assistance client for employment or training is to
    A. give him self-confidence
    B. make him self-supporting
    C. have him learn a new trade
    D. take him off the streets

19. ____

20. Sometimes clients become silent during interviews.
    Of the following, the MOST probable reason for such silence is that the client is
    A. getting ready to tell a lie
    B. of low intelligence and does not know the answers to your questions
    C. thinking things over or has nothing more to say on the subject
    D. wishing he were not on welfare

20. ____

KEY (CORRECT ANSWERS)

1. D	6. D	11. B	16. B
2. B	7. B	12. D	17. A
3. A	8. C	13. C	18. C
4. C	9. A	14. D	19. B
5. C	10. C	15. A	20. C

EXAMINATION SECTION
TEST 1

DIRECTIONS: Each question or incomplete statement is followed by several suggested answers or completions. Select the l one that BEST answers the question or completes the statement. *PRINT THE LETTER OF THE CORRECT ANSWER IN THE SPACE AT THE RIGHT.*

1. The applicant you are interviewing is a man in his late forties who has recently lost his job and has a family of eight to support. He is very upset and tells you he does not know where he will get the money to purchase food for the family and pay the rent. He does not know what he will do if he is found not eligible for public assistance. He asks you whether you think he will be eligible. You feel the applicant has a good chance, and you think he should receive financial assistance, but you are not completely certain that he is eligible for public assistance under departmental policy.
   Of the following, the BEST action for you to take is to

   A. reassure the applicant and tell him you are sure everything will be all right because there is no sense in worrying him before you know for certain that he is not eligible
   B. tell the applicant that as far as you are concerned he should receive public assistance but that you are not certain the department will go along with your recommendation
   C. tell the applicant that you are not sure that he will be found eligible for public assistance
   D. adopt a cool manner and tell the applicant that he must behave like an adult and not allow himself to become emotional about the situation

1._____

2. When conducting an interview with a client receiving public assistance, it would be LEAST important for you to try to

   A. understand the reasons for the client's statements
   B. conduct the interview on the client's intellectual level
   C. imitate the client's speech as much as possible
   D. impress the client with the agency's concern for his welfare

2._____

Questions 3-6.

DIRECTIONS: Questions 3 through 6 are to be answered SOLELY on basis of the following case history of the Foster family.

FOSTER CASE HISTORY

Form W-341-C
Rev. 3/1/03
600M-804077-S-200 (93)-245

Date: Jan. 25, 2015
Case Name: Foster
Case No. : ADC-3415968

Family Composition: Ann Foster, b. 7.23.77
Gerry b. 1.7.02
Susan b. 4.1.04
John b. 5.3.07
Joan b. 10.14.10

Mrs. Foster was widowed in June 2011 when her husband was killed in a car accident. Since that time, the family has received public assistance. Mrs. Foster has been referred for housekeeping service by the Social Service Department of Lincoln Hospital, where she is being treated in the neurology clinic. Her primary diagnosis is multiple sclerosis. The hospital reports that she is going through a period of deterioration characterized by an unsteady gait, and weakness and tremor in the limbs. At this time, her capacity to manage a household and four children is severely limited. She feels quite overwhelmed and is unable to function adequately in taking care of her home.

In addition to the medical reasons, it is advisable that a housekeeper be placed in the home as part of a total plan to avoid further family breakdown and deterioration. This deterioration is reflected by all family members. Mrs. Foster is severely depressed and is unable to meet the needs of her children, who have a variety of problems. Joan, the youngest, is not speaking, is hyperactive, and in general is not developing normally for a child her age. John is showing learning problems in school and has poor articulation. Susan was not promoted last year and is a behavior problem at home. Gerry, the oldest, is deformed due to a fire at age two. It is clear that Mrs. Foster cannot control or properly discipline her children, but even more important is the fact that she is unable to offer them the encouragement and guidance they require.

It is hoped that providing housekeeping service will relieve Mrs. Foster of the basic household chores so that she will be less frustrated and better able to provide the love and guidance needed by her children.

3. The age of the child who is described as not developing normally, hyperactive, and not speaking is

A. 4 B. 7 C. 10 D. 13

4. Which of the following CANNOT be verified on the basis of the Foster Case History above?

A. William Foster was Ann Foster's husband.
B. Mrs. Foster has been seen in the neurology clinic at Lincoln Hospital.
C. John Foster has trouble with his speech.
D. The Foster family has received public assistance since June 2011.

5. The form on which the information about the Foster family is presented is known as

A. Family Composition Form
B. Form Rev. 3/1/03
C. Form W-341-C
D. ADC-3415968

6. According to the above case history, housekeeping service is being requested PRIMARILY because

   A. no one in the family can perform the household chores
   B. Mrs. Foster suffers from multiple sclerosis and requires assistance with the household chores
   C. the children are exhibiting behavior problems resulti from the mother's illness
   D. the children have no father

7. You notice that an applicant whom you rejected for public assistance is back at the center the following morning and is waiting to be interviewed by another worker in your group.
   Of the following, the BEST approach for you to take is to

   A. inform the worker, before she interviews the applicant that you had interviewed and rejected him the previous day
   B. not inform the worker about the situation and let her make her own decision
   C. approach the applicant and tell him he was rejected for good reason and will have to leave the center immediately
   D. ask the special officer at the center to remove the applicant

8. You have just finished interviewing an applicant who has a violent temper and has displayed a great amount of hostility toward you during the interview. You find he is ineligible for public assistance. Departmental policy is that all applicants are notified by mail in a day or so of their acceptance or rejection for public assistance. However, you also have the option, if you think it is desirable, of notifying the applicant at the interview.
   Of the following, the BEST action for you to take in this case is to

   A. tell the applicant of his rejection during the interview
   B. have the applicant notified of the results of the interview by mail only
   C. ask your supervisor to inform the applicant of his rejection
   D. inform the applicant of the results of the interview, with a special patrolman at your side

9. You are interviewing a client who speaks English poorly and whose native language is Spanish. Your knowledge of Spanish is very limited.
   Of the following, the FIRST action it would be best for you to take is to

   A. try to locate a worker at the center who speaks Spanish
   B. write our your questions because it is easier for people to understand a new language when it is written rather than when it is spoken
   C. do the best you can, using hand gestures to make yourself understood
   D. tell the client to return with a friend or relative who speaks English

10. During an interview with a client of another race, he accuses you of racial prejudice and asks for an interviewer of his own race.
    Of the following, which is the BEST way to handle the situation?

    A. In a friendly manner, tell the client that eligibility is based on the regulations and the facts, not on prejudice, and ask him to continue with the interview.
    B. Explain to your supervisor that you cannot deal with someone who accuses you of prejudice, and ask your supervisor to assign the client someone of his own race.
    C. Assure the client that you will lean over backwards to treat his application favorably.

D. Tell the client that some of your friends are of his race and that you could therefore not possibly be prejudiced.

Questions 11-15.

DIRECTIONS: In order to answer Questions 11 through 15, assume that you have been asked to write a short report on the basis of the information contained in the following passage about the granting of emergency funds to the Smith family.

Mr. and Mrs. Smith, who have been receiving public assistance for the last six months, arrive at the center the morning of August 2, totally upset and anxious because they and their family have been burned out of their apartment the night before. The fire seems to have been of suspicious origin because at the time it broke out witnesses spotted two neighborhood teenagers running away from the scene. The policemen, who arrived at the scene shortly after the firemen, took down the pertinent information about the alleged arsonists.

The Smiths have spent the night with friends but now request emergency housing and emergency funds for themselves and their four children to purchase food and to replace the clothing which was destroyed by the fire. The burned-out apartment had consisted of 5 rooms and a bath, and the Smiths are now worried that they will be forced to accept smaller accommodations. Furthermore, since Mrs. Smith suffers from a heart murmur, she is worried that their new living quarters will necessitate her climbing too many stairs. Her previous apartment was a one-flight walk-up, which was acceptable.

As the worker in charge, you have studied the case, determined the amount of the emergency grant, made temporary arrangements for the Smiths to stay at a hotel, and reassured Mrs. Smith that everything possible will be done to find them an apartment which will meet with their approval.

11. Which of the following would it be BEST to include in the report as the reason for the emergency grant?   11.____

    A. The police have decided that the fire is of suspicious origin.
    B. Two neighborhood teenagers were seen leaving the fire at the Smiths'.
    C. The apartment of the Smith family has been destroyed by fire.
    D. Mrs. Smith suffers from a heart murmur and cannot climb stairs.

12. Which of the following would it be BEST to accept as verification of the fire?   12.____
    A

    A. letter from the friends with whom the Smiths stayed the previous night
    B. photograph of the fire
    C. dated newspaper clipping describing the fire
    D. note from the Smiths' neighbors

13. A report of the Smith family's need for a new apartment must be sent to the center's housing specialist.   13.____
    Which of the following recommendations for housing would be MOST appropriate?

    A. Two bedrooms, first floor walk-up
    B. Five rooms, ground floor
    C. Two-room suite, hotel with elevator
    D. Three rooms, building with elevator

14. For which of the following are the Smiths requesting emergency funds? 14.____

   A. Furniture   B. Food
   C. A hotel room   D. Repairs in their apartment

15. Which of the following statements provides the BEST summary of the action taken by you on the Smith case and is MOST important for inclusion in your report? 15.____

   A. Mr. and Mrs. Smith arrived upset and anxious and were reassured.
   B. It was verified that there was a fire.
   C. Temporary living arrangements were made, and the amount of the emergency grant was determined.
   D. The case was studied and a new apartment was found for the Smiths which met with their approval.

16. It is important that you remember what has happened between you and a client during an interview so that you may deliver appropriate services. 16.____
   However, the one of the following which is the MOST likely reason that taking notes during the interview may not always be a good practice is that

   A. you may lose the notes and have to go back and see the client again
   B. some clients may believe that you are not interested in what they are saying
   C. you are the only one who is likely to read the notes
   D. some clients may believe that you are not smart enough to remember what happened in the interview

17. Before an applicant seeking public assistance can be interviewed, he must fill out a complex application form which consists of eleven pages of questions requesting very detailed information. 17.____
   Of the following, the BEST time for you to review the information on the application form is

   A. before she begins to interview the applicant
   B. after she has asked the applicant a few questions to put him at ease
   C. towards the end of the interview so that she has a chance to think about the information received during the interview
   D. after the interview has been completed

Questions 18-20.

DIRECTIONS: In Questions 18 through 20, choose the lettered word which means MOST NEARLY the same as the underlined word in the sentence.

18. He needed public assistance because he was incapacitated. The word incapacitated means MOST NEARLY 18.____

   A. uneducated   B. disabled
   C. uncooperative D. discharged

19. The caseworker explained to the client that signing the document was compulsory. The word compulsory means MOST NEARLY 19.____

   A. temporary B. required
   C. different D. comprehensive

20. The woman's actions did not <u>jeopardize</u> her eligibility for benefits. 20.____
    The word <u>jeopardize</u> means MOST NEARLY

    A. delay   B. reinforce   C. determine   D. endanger

KEY (CORRECT ANSWERS)

1.	C	11.	C
2.	C	12.	C
3.	A	13.	B
4.	A	14.	B
5.	C	15.	C
6.	B	16.	B
7.	A	17.	A
8.	B	18.	B
9.	A	19.	B
10.	A	20.	D

TEST 2

DIRECTIONS: Each question or incomplete statement is followed by several suggested answers or completions. Select the one that BEST answers the question or completes the statement. *PRINT THE LETTER OF THE CORRECT ANSWER IN THE SPACE AT THE RIGHT.*

Questions 1-4.

DIRECTIONS: Questions 1 through 4 are to be answered on the basis of the information given in the Fact Situation and Sample Form below.

FACT SITUATION

On October 7, 2014, John Smith (Case #ADC-U 1467912) applied and was accepted for public assistance for himself and his family. His family consists of his wife, Helen, and their children: William, age 9; John Jr., age 6; and Mary, age 2. The family has lived in a five-room apartment located at 142 West 137 Street, Manhattan, since July 18, 2008. Mr. Smith signed a 2-year lease for this apartment on July 18, 2014 at a rent of $500 per month. The maximum rental allowance for a family of this size is $420 per month. Utilities are included in this rent-controlled multiple dwelling.

Since the cost of renting this apartment is in excess of the allowable amount, the Supervising Clerk (Income Maintenance) is required to fill out a "Request for Approval of Exception to Policy for Shelter Allowance/Rehousing Expenses."

A sample of a section of this form follows.

SAMPLE FORM

REQUEST FOR APPROVAL OF EXCEPTION TO POLICY FOR SHELTER ALLOWANCE /REHOUSING EXPENSES

Case Name	Case No. or Pending		Acceptance Date	Group No.	
Present Address ZIP	Apt. No. or Location	No. of Rooms	Rent per Mo. $	Occupancy Date	
HOUSEHOLD COMPOSITION (List all persons living in the household) Column I Surname First	Col. 2 Birth-date	Col. 3 Sex	Column 4 Relation to Case Head	Column 5 Marital Status	Column 6 P. A. Status

1. Based on the information given in the Fact Situation, which one of the following should be entered in the space for *Occupancy Date?*

   A. October 7, 2014
   B. July 18, 2014
   C. July 18, 2008
   D. Unknown

2. What amount should be entered in the space labeled *Rent per Mo.?*

   A. $500   B. $420   C. $300   D. $80

3. Based on the information given in the Fact Situation, it is IMPOSSIBLE to fill in which one of the following blanks?

   A. *Case Number or pending*
   B. *Acceptance Date*
   C. *Apt. No. or Location*
   D. *No. of Rooms*

4. Which of the following should be entered in Column 4 for Helen Smith?

   A. Wife   B. Head   C. Mother   D. Unknown

Questions 5-13.

DIRECTIONS: In Questions 5 through 13, perform the computations indicated and choose the CORRECT answer from the four choices given.

5. Add $4.34, $34.50, $6.00, $101.76, $90.67. From the result, subtract $60.54 and $10.56.

   A. $76.17   B. $156.37   C. $166.17   D. $300.37

6. Add 2,200, 2,600, 252, and 47.96.
   From the result, subtract 202.70, 1,200, 2,150, and 434.43.

   A. 1,112.83   B. 1,213.46   C. 1,341.51   D. 1,348.91

7. Multiply 1850 by .05 and multiply 3300 by .08 and then add both results.

   A. 242.50   B. 264.00   C. 333.25   D. 356.50

8. Multiply 312.77 by .04.
   Round off the result to the nearest hundredth.

   A. 12.52   B. 12.511   C. 12.518   D. 12.51

9. Add 362.05, 91.13, 347.81, and 17.46, and then divide the result by 6.
   The answer rounded off to the nearest hundredth is

   A. 138.409   B. 137.409   C. 136.41   D. 136.40

10. Add 66.25 and 15.06, and then multiply the result by 2 1/6.
    The answer is MOST NEARLY

    A. 176.18   B. 176.17   C. 162.66   D. 162.62

11. Each of the following options contains three decimals. In which case do all three decimals have the same value?

    A. .3; .30; .03
    B. .25; .250; .2500
    C. 1.9; 1.90; 1.09
    D. .35; .350; .035

12. Add 1/2 the sum of (539.84 and 479.26) to 1/3 the sum of (1461.93 and 927.27). Round off the result to the nearest whole number.

    A. 3408 B. 2899 C. 1816 D. 1306

13. Multiply $5,906.09 by 15%, and then divide the result by 1/3.

    A. $295.30 B. $885.91 C. $8,859.14 D. $29,530.45

Questions 14-18.

DIRECTIONS: Questions 14 through 18 are to be answered SOLELY on the basis of the information provided in the following passage.

The ideal relationship for the interview is one of mutual confidence. To try to pretend, to put on a front of cordiality and friendship is extremely unwise for the interviewer because he will certainly convey, by subtle means, his real feelings. It is the interviewer's responsibility to take the lead in establishing a relationship of mutual confidence.

As the interviewer, you should help the interviewee to feel at ease and ready to talk. One of the best ways to do this is to be at ease yourself. If you are, it will probably be evident; if you are not, it will almost certainly be apparent to the interviewee.

Begin the interview with topics for discussion which are easy to talk about and non-menacing. This interchange can be like the conversation of people when they are waiting for a bus, at the ball game, or discussing the weather. However, do not prolong this warm-up too long since the interviewee knows as well as you do that these are not the things he came to discuss. Delaying too long in getting down to business may suggest to him that you are reluctant to deal with the topic.

Once you get onto the main topics, do all that you can to get the interviewee to talk freely with as little prodding from you as possible. This will probably require that you give him some idea of the area, and of ways of looking at it. Avoid, however, prejudicing or coloring his remarks by what you say; especially, do not in any way indicate that there are certain things you want to hear, others which you do not want to hear. It is essential that he feel free to express his own ideas unhampered by your ideas, your values and preconceptions.

Do not appear to dominate the interview, nor have even the suggestion of a patronizing attitude. Ask some questions which will enable the interviewee to take pride in his knowledge. Take the attitude that the interviewee sincerely wants the interview to achieve its purpose. This creates a warm, permissive atmosphere that is most important in all interviews.

14. Of the following, the BEST title for the above passage is

    A. PERMISSIVENESS IN INTERVIEWING
    B. INTERVIEWING TECHNIQUES
    C. THE FACTOR OF PRETENSE IN THE INTERVIEW
    D. THE CORDIAL INTERVIEW

15. Which of the following recommendations on the conduct of an interview is made by the above passage?

    A. Conduct the interview as if it were an interchange between people discussing the weather.
    B. The interview should be conducted in a highly impersonal manner.
    C. Allow enough time for the interview so that the interviewee does not feel rushed.
    D. Start the interview with topics which are not threatening to the interviewee.

16. The above passage indicates that the interviewer should

    A. feel free to express his opinions
    B. patronize the interviewee and display a permissive attitude
    C. permit the interviewee to give the needed information in his own fashion
    D. provide for privacy when conducting the interview

17. The meaning of the word *unhampered,* as it is used in the last sentence of the fourth paragraph of the preceding passage, is MOST NEARLY

    A. unheeded   B. unobstructed
    C. hindered   D. aided

18. It can be INFERRED from the above passage that

    A. interviewers, while generally mature, lack confidence
    B. certain methods in interviewing are more successful than others in obtaining information
    C. there is usually a reluctance on the part of interviewers to deal with unpleasant topics
    D. it is best for the interviewer not to waiver from the use of hard and fast rules when dealing with clients

19. The applicant whom you are interviewing is not talking rationally, and he admits that he is under the influence of alcohol.
    Which of the following is the BEST way of handling this situation?

    A. Call a security guard and have the applicant removed.
    B. Tell the applicant that unless he gets control of himself, he will not receive financial assistance.
    C. Send out for a cup of black coffee for the applicant.
    D. End the interview and plan to schedule another appointment.

20. During an interview, an applicant who has submitted an application for assistance breaks down and cries. Of the following, the BEST way of handling this situation is to

    A. end the interview and schedule a new appointment
    B. be patient and sympathetic, and encourage the applicant to continue the interview
    C. tell the applicant sternly that crying will not help matters
    D. tell the applicant that you will do everything you can to get the application approved

KEY (CORRECT ANSWERS)

1. C
2. A
3. C
4. A
5. C

6. A
7. D
8. D
9. C
10. B

11. B
12. D
13. A
14. B
15. D

16. C
17. B
18. B
19. D
20. B

EXAMINATION SECTION

TEST 1

DIRECTIONS: Each question or incomplete statement is followed by several suggested answers or completions. Select the one that BEST answers the question or completes the statement. *PRINT THE LETTER OF THE CORRECT ANSWER IN THE SPACE AT THE RIGHT.*

1. When a worker is planning a future interview with a client, of the following, the MOST important consideration is the
   A. recommendations he will make to the client
   B. place where the client will be interviewed
   C. purpose for which the client will be interviewed
   D. personality of the client

2. For a worker to make a practice of reviewing the client's case record, if available, prior to the interview is usually
   A. *inadvisable*, because knowledge of the client's past record will tend to influence the worker's judgment
   B. *advisable*, because knowledge of the client's background will help the worker to identify discrepancies in the client's responses
   C. *inadvisable*, because such review is time-consuming and of questionable value
   D. *advisable*, because knowledge of the client's background will help the worker to understand the client's situation

3. Assume that a worker makes a practice of constantly re-assuring clients with serious and complex problems by making such statements as: *I'm sure you'll soon be well; I know you'll get a job soon*; or *Everything will be all right.*
   Of the following, the MOST likely result of such practice is to
   A. encourage the client and make him feel that the worker understands what the client is going through
   B. make the client doubtful about the worker's understanding of his difficulties and the worker's ability to help
   C. confuse the client and cause him to hesitate to take any action on his own initiative
   D. help the client to be more realistic about his situation and the probability that it will improve

4. In order to get the maximum amount of information from a client during an interview, of the following, it is MOST important for the worker to communicate to the client the feeling that the worker is
   A. interested in the client
   B. a figure of authority
   C. efficient in his work habits
   D. sympathetic to the client's lifestyle

5. Of the following, the worker who takes extremely detailed notes during an interview with a client is MOST likely to
   A. encourage the client to talk freely
   B. distract and antagonize the client
   C. help the client feel at ease
   D. understand the client's feelings

6. You find that many of the clients you interview are verbally abusive and unusually hostile to you.
   Of the following, the MOST appropriate action for you to take FIRST is to
   A. review your interviewing techniques and consider whether you may be provoking these clients
   B. act in a more authoritative manner when interviewing troublesome clients
   C. tell these clients that you will not process their applications unless their troublesome behavior ceases
   D. disregard the clients' troublesome behavior during the interviews

7. During an interview, you did not completely understand several of your client's responses. In each instance, you rephrased the client's statement and asked the client if that was what he meant.
   For you to use such a technique during interviews would be considered
   A. *inappropriate*; you may have distorted the client's meaning by rephrasing his statements
   B. *inappropriate*; you should have asked the same question until you received a comprehensible response
   C. *appropriate*; the client will have a chance to correct you if you have misinterpreted his responses
   D. *appropriate*; a worker should rephrase clients' responses for the records

8. A worker is interviewing a client who has just had a severe emotional shock because of an assault on her by a mugger.
   Of the following, the approach which would generally be MOST helpful to the client is for the worker to
   A. comfort the client and encourage her to talk about the assault
   B. sympathize with the client but refuse to talk about the assault
   C. tell the client to control her emotions and think positively about the future
   D. proceed with the interview in an impersonal and unemotional manner

9. A worker finds that her questions are misinterpreted by many of the clients she interviews.
   Of the following, the MOST likely reason for this problem is that the
   A. client is not listening attentively
   B. client wants to avoid the subject being discussed
   C. worker has failed to express her meaning clearly
   D. worker has failed to put the client at ease

10. For a worker to look directly at the client and observe him during the interview is, generally,
    A. *inadvisable*; this will make the client nervous and uncomfortable
    B. *advisable*; the client will be more likely to refrain from lying
    C. *inadvisable*; the worker will not be able to take notes for the case record
    D. *advisable*; this will encourage conversation and accelerate the progress of the interview

11. You are interviewing a client who is applying for social services for the first time. In order to encourage this client to freely give you the information needed for you to establish his eligibility, of the following, the BEST way to start the interview is by
    A. asking questions the client can easily answer
    B. conveying the impression that his responses to your questions will be checked
    C. asking two or three similar but important questions
    D. assuring the client that your sole responsibility is *getting the facts*

12. Workers are encouraged to record significant information obtained from clients and services provided for clients.
    Of the following, the MOST important reason for this practice is that these case records will
    A. help to reduce the need for regular supervisory conferences
    B. indicate to workers which clients are taking up the most time
    C. provide information which will help the agency to improve its services to clients
    D. make it easier to verify the complaints of clients

13. As a worker in the employment eligibility section, you find that interviews can be completed in a shorter period of time if you ask questions which limit the client to a certain answer.
    For you to use such a technique would be considered
    A. *inappropriate*, because this type of question usually requires advance preparation
    B. *inappropriate*, because this type of question may inhibit the client from saying what he really means
    C. *appropriate*, because you know the areas into which the questions should be directed
    D. *appropriate*, because this type of question usually helps clients to express themselves clearly

14. Assume that a worker at a juvenile detention center is planning foster care placement for a child.
    For the worker to have the child participate in the planning is generally considered to be
    A. time-consuming and of little practical value in preparing the child for placement
    B. valuable in helping the child adjust to future placement

C. useful, because the child will be more likely to cooperate with others in the center
D. anxiety-provoking because the child will feel that he has been abandoned

15. You have been assigned to interview the mother of a five-year-old son in her home to get information useful in locating the child's absent father. During the interview, you notice many serious bruises on the child's arms and legs, which the mother explains are due to the child's clumsiness.
    Of the following, your BEST course of action is to
    A. accept the mother's explanation and concentrate on getting information which will help you to locate the father
    B. advise the mother to have the child examined for a medical condition that may be causing his clumsiness
    C. make a surprise visit to the mother later, to see whether someone is beating the child
    D. complete your interview with the mother and report the case to your supervisor for investigation of possible child abuse

15.____

16. During an interview, the former landlord of an absent father offers to help you to locate the father if you will give the landlord confidential information you have on the financial situation of the father.
    Of the following, you should
    A. immediately end the interview with the landlord
    B. urge the landlord to help you but explain that you are not permitted to give him confidential information
    C. freely give the landlord the confidential information he requests about the father
    D. give the landlord the information only if he promises to keep it confidential

16.____

17. You feel that your client, a released mental patient, is not adjusting well to living on his own in an apartment. To gather more information, you interview privately his next-door neighbor, who claims that the client is creating a disturbance and speaks of the client in an angry and insulting manner.
    Of the following, the BEST action for you to take in this situation is to
    A. listen patiently to the neighbor to try to get the facts about your client's behavior
    B. inform the neighbor that he has no right to speak insultingly about a mentally ill person
    C. make an appointment to interview the neighbor some other time when he isn't so upset
    D. tell the neighbor that you were not aware of the client's behavior and that you will have the client moved

17.____

18. As a worker assigned to an income maintenance center, you are interviewing a client to determine his eligibility for a work program. Suddenly, the client begins to shout that he is in no condition to work and that you are persecuting him for no reason.

18.____

Of the following, your BEST response to this client is to
- A. advise the client to stop shouting or you will call for the security guard
- B. wait until the client calms down, then order him to come back for another interview
- C. insist that you are not persecuting the client and that he must complete the interview
- D. wait until the client calms down, say that you understand how he feels, and try to continue the interview

19. You are counseling a mother whose 17-year-old son has recently been returned home from a mental institution. Although she is willing to care for her son at home, she is frightened by his strange and sometimes violent behavior and does not know the best arrangement to make for his care.
Of the following, your MOST appropriate response to this mother's problem is to
    - A. describe the supportive services and alternatives to home care which are available
    - B. help her to accept her son's strange and violent behavior
    - C. tell her that she will not be permitted to care for her son at home if she is frightened by his behavior
    - D. convince her that she is not responsible for her son's mental condition

20. Assume that, as an intake worker, you are interviewing an elderly man who comes to the center several times a month to discuss topics with you which are not related to social service. You realize that the man is lonely and enjoys these conversations.
Of the following, it would be MOST appropriate to
    - A. politely discourage the man from coming in to pass the time with you
    - B. avoid speaking to this man the next time he comes into the center
    - C. explore with the client his feelings about joining a Senior Citizens' Center
    - D. continue to hold these conversations with the man

21. A client you are interviewing in the housing elibility section tends to ramble on after each response that he gives, so that man clients are kept waiting.
In this situation, of the following, it would be MOST advisable to
    - A. try to direct the interview, in order to obtain the necessary information
    - B. reduce the number of questions asked so that you can shorten the interview
    - C. arrange a second interview for the client so that you can give him more time
    - D. tell the client that he is wasting everybody's time

22. A non-minority worker in an employment eligibility unit is about to interview a minority client on public assistance for job placement when the client says: *What does your kind know about my problems? You've never had to survive out on these streets.*
Of the following, the worker's MOST appropriate response to this situation is to

6 (#1)

   A. postpone the interview until a minority worker is available to interview the client
   B. tell the client that he must cooperate with the worker if he wants to continue receiving public assistance
   C. explain to the client the function of the worker in this unit and the services he provides
   D. assure the client that you do not have to be a member of a minority group to understand the effects of poverty

23. As a worker in a family services unit, you have been assigned to follow-up a case folder recently forwarded from the protective-diagnostic unit.
   After making appropriate clerical notations in your records such as name of client and date of receipt, which of the following would be the MOST appropriate step to take next?
   A. Confer with your supervisor
   B. Read and review all reports included in the case folder
   C. Arrange to visit with the client at his home
   D. Confer with representatives of any other agencies which have been in contact with the client

24. As a worker in the employment section, you are interviewing a young client who seriously underestimates the amount of education and training he will require for a certain occupation.
   For you to tell the client that you think he is mistaken would, generally, be considered
   A. *inadvisable*, because workers should not express their opinions to clients
   B. *inadvisable*, because clients have the right to self-determination
   C. *advisable*, because clients should generally be alerted to their misconceptions
   D. *advisable*, because workers should convince clients to adopt a proper lifestyle

25. As an intake worker, you are counseling a mother and her unmarried, thirteen-year-old daughter, who is six months pregnant, concerning the advisability of placing the daughter's baby for adoption. The mother insists on adoption, but the daughter remains silent and appears undecided.
   Of the following, you should encourage the daughter to
   A. make the final decision on adoption herself
   B. keep her baby despite her mother's insistence on adoption
   C. accept her mother's insistence on adoption
   D. make the decision on adoption together with her mother

KEY (CORRECT ANSWERS)

1.	C	11.	A
2.	D	12.	C
3.	B	13.	B
4.	A	14.	B
5.	B	15.	D
6.	A	16.	B
7.	C	17.	A
8.	A	18.	D
9.	C	19.	A
10.	D	20.	C

21. A
22. C
23. B
24. C
25. D

TEST 2

DIRECTIONS: Each question or incomplete statement is followed by several suggested answers or completions. Select the one that BEST answers the question or completes the statement. *PRINT THE LETTER OF THE CORRECT ANSWER IN THE SPACE AT THE RIGHT.*

1. You are interviewing a legally responsible absent father who refuses to make child support payments because he claims the mother physically abuses the child.
   Of the following, the BEST way for you to handle his situation is to tell the father that you
   A. will report his complaint about the mother, but he is still responsible for making child support payments
   B. suspect that he is complaining about the mother in order to avoid his own responsibility for making child support payments
   C. are concerned with his responsibility to make child support payments, not with the mother's abuse of the child
   D. cannot determine his responsibility for making child support payments until his complaint about the mother is investigated

   1.____

2. On a visit to a home where child abuse is alleged, you find the mother preparing lunch for her two children. She tells you that she knows that a neighbor is spreading lies about her treatment of the children.
   Which one of the following is the BEST action for you to take?
   A. Thank the mother for her assistance, leave the home, and indicate in your report that the allegation of child abuse is false
   B. Tell the mother that, since you have been sent to visit her, there must be some truth to the allegations
   C. Explain the purpose of your visit and observe whatever interaction takes place between the children and the mother
   D. Conclude the interview, since you have observed the mother preparing a good lunch for the children

   2.____

3. You are interviewing an elderly woman who lives alone to determine her eligibility for homemaker service at public expense. Though obviously frail and in need of this service, the woman is not completely cooperative, and, during the interview, is often silent for a considerable period of time.
   Of the following, the BEST way for you to deal with these periods of silence is to
   A. realize that she may be embarrassed to have to apply for homemaker service at public expense, and emphasize her right to this service
   B. postpone the interview and make an appointment with her for a later date, when she may be better able to cooperate
   C. explain to the woman that you have many clients to interview and need her cooperation to complete the interview quickly
   D. recognize that she is probably hiding something and begin to ask questions to draw her out

   3.____

4. During a conference with an adolescent boy at a juvenile detention center, you find out for the first time that he would prefer to be placed in foster care rather than return to his natural parents.
To uncover the reasons why the boy dislikes his own home, of the following, it would be MOST advisable for you to
   A. ask the boy a number of short, simple questions about his feelings
   B. encourage the boy to talk freely and express his feelings as best he can
   C. interview the parents and find out why the boy doesn't want to live at home
   D. administer a battery of psychological tests in order to make an assessment of the boy's problems

1.____

5. Of the following, the BEST way to determine which activities should be provided for members of a Senior Citizens' Center is to
   A. ask the neighborhood community board to submit their recommendations
   B. meet with the professional staff of the center to get their opinions
   C. encourage the members of the center to express their personal preferences
   D. study the schedules prepared by other Senior Citizens' Centers for guidance

5.____

6. You are interviewing a mother who is applying for Aid to Families with Dependent Children because the husband has deserted the family. The mother becomes annoyed at having to answer your questions and tells you to leave her apartment.
Which one of the following actions would be MOST appropriate to take FIRST in this situation?
   A. Return to the office and close the case for lack of cooperation
   B. Tell the mother that you will get the information from her neighbors if she does not cooperate
   C. Tell the mother that you must stay until you get answers to your questions
   D. Explain to the mother the reasons for the interview and the consequences of her failure to cooperate

6.____

7. A worker assigned to visit homebound clients to determine their eligibility for Medicaid must understand each client's situation as completely as possible.
Of the following source which may provide insight into the client's situation, the one that is generally MOST revealing is:
   A. Close relatives of the client, who have known him for many years
   B. Next-door neighbors, who have observed the daily living habits of the client
   C. The client himself, who can provide his own description of his situation
   D. The records of other social agencies that may have served the client

7.____

8. A worker counseling juvenile clients finds that, although he can tolerate most of their behavior, he becomes infuriated when they lie to him.
Of the following, the worker can BEST deal with his anger at his clients' lying by

8.____

A. recognizing his feelings of anger and learning to control expression of these feelings to his clients
B. warning his clients that he cannot be responsible for his anger when a client lies to him
C. using willpower to suppress his feelings of anger when a client lies to him
D. realizing that lying is a common trait of juveniles and not directed against him personally

9. During an interview at the employment eligibility section, one of your clients, a former drug addict, has expressed an interest in attending a community counseling center and resuming his education.
In this case, the MOST appropriate action that you should take FIRST is to
    A. determine whether this ambition is realistic for a former drug addict
    B. send the client's application to a community counseling center which provides services to former addicts
    C. ask the client whether he is really motivated or is just seeking your approval
    D. encourage and assist the client to take this step, since his interest is a positive sign

10. Because of habitual neglect by his mother, a five-year-old boy has been placed in a foster home.
For the worker to encourage the mother to visit the boy in the foster home is, generally,
    A. *desirable*, because the boy will be helped by continuing his ties with his mother
    B. *undesirable*, because the boy will be upset by his mother's visits and will have a harder time adjusting to the foster home
    C. *desirable*, because the mother will learn from the foster parents how she should treat the boy
    D. *undesirable*, because the mother should be punished for her neglect of the boy by complete separation from him

11. You are interviewing a client who, during previous appointments, has not responded to your requests for information required to determine his continued eligibility for services. On this occasion, the client again offers an excuse which you feel is not acceptable.
For you to advise the client of the probable loss of services because of his lack of cooperation is
    A. *inappropriate*, because the threat to withhold services will harm the relationship between worker and client
    B. *inappropriate*, because workers should not reveal to clients that they do not believe their statements
    C. *appropriate*, because social services are a reward given to cooperative clients
    D. *appropriate*, because the worker should inform clients of the consequences of their lack of cooperation

12. Assume that you are counseling an adolescent boy in a juvenile detention center who has been a ringleader in smuggling pot into the center. During your regular interview with this boy, of the following, it would be *advisable* to
    A. tell him you know that he has been involved in smuggling pot and that you are trying to understand the reasons for his misbehavior
    B. ignore his pot smuggling in order to reassure him that you understand and accept him, even though you do not agree with his standards of behavior
    C. warn him that you have reported his pot smuggling and that he will be punished for his misbehavior
    D. show him that you disagree of his pot smuggling, but assure him that you will not report him for his misbehavior

13. Your unit has received several complaints about a homeless elderly woman living outdoors in various locations in the area. To help determine the need for protective services for this woman, you interview several persons in the neighborhood who are familiar with her, but all are uncooperative or reluctant to give information.
    Of the following, your BEST approach to these persons is to explain to them that
    A. you will take legal steps against them if they do not cooperate with you
    B. their cooperation may enable you to help this homeless woman
    C. you need their cooperation to remove this homeless woman from their neighborhood
    D. they will be responsible for any harm that comes to this homeless woman

14. A foster mother complains to the worker that a ten-year-old boy placed with her is overaggressive and unmanageable. The worker, knowing that the boy has been placed unsuccessfully several times before, constantly reassures the foster mother that the boy is improving steadily.
    For the worker to do this, generally,
    A. *good practice*, because the foster mother may accept the professional opinion of the worker and keep the boy
    B. *poor practice*, because the foster mother may be discouraged from discussing the boy's problems with the worker
    C. *good practice*, because the foster mother may feel guilty if she gives up the boy when he is improving
    D. *poor practice*, because the boy should not remain with a foster mother who complains about his behavior

15. Assume that, as a worker in the liaison and adjustment unit, you are interviewing a client regarding an adjustment in budget. The client begins to scream at you that she holds you responsible for the decrease in her allowance.
    Of the following, which is the BEST way for you to handle this situation?
    A. Attempt to discuss the matter calmly with the client and explain her right to a hearing
    B. Urge the client to appeal and assure her of your support

C. Tell the client that her disorderly behavior will be held against her
D. Tell the client that the reduction is due to red tape and is not your fault

16. As a worker assigned to a juvenile detention center, you are having a counseling interview with a recently admitted boy who is having serious problems in adjusting to confinement in the center. During the interview, the boy frequently interrupts to ask you personal questions.
Of the following, the BEST way for you to deal with these questions is to
    A. tell him in a friendly way that your job is to discuss his problems, not yours
    B. try to understand how the questions relate to the boy's own problems and reply with discretion
    C. take no notice of the questions and continue with the interview
    D. try to win the boy's confidence by answering his questions in detail

16.____

17. A worker is interviewing an elderly woman who hesitates to provide necessary information about her finances to determine whether she is eligible for supplementary assistance. She fears that this information will be reported to others and that her neighbors will find out that she is destitute and applying for welfare.
Of the following, the worker's MOST appropriate response is to
    A. tell her that, if she hesitates to give this information, the agency will get it from other sources
    B. assure her that this information is kept strictly confidential, and will not be given to unauthorized persons
    C. convince her that her application will be turned down unless she provides this information as soon as possible
    D. ask for the name and address of her nearest relative and obtain the information from that person

17.____

18. You are counseling a couple whose children have been placed in a foster home because of the couple's quarrelling and child neglect. When you interview the wife by herself, she tells you that she knows the husband often cheats on her with other women, but she is too afraid of the husband's temper to tell him how much this hurts her.
For you to immediately reveal to the husband the wife's unhappiness concerning his cheating is, generally,
    A. *good practice*, because it will help the husband to understand why his wife quarrels with him
    B. *poor practice*, because information received from the wife should not be given to the husband without her permission
    C. *good practice*, because the husband will direct his anger at you rather than at his wife
    D. *poor practice*, because the wife may have told you a false story about her husband in order to win your sympathy

18.____

6 (#2)

19. A worker in an employment eligibility section is beginning a job placement interview with a tall, strongly-built young man. As the man sits down, the worker comments: *I know a big fellow like you wouldn't be interested in any clerical job.*
    For the worker to make such a comment is, generally,
    A. *appropriate*, because it creates an air of familiarity which may put the man at ease
    B. *inappropriate*, because the man may be sensitive about his physical size
    C. *appropriate*, because the worker is using his judgment to help speed up the interview
    D. *inappropriate*, because the man may feel he is being pressured into agreeing with the worker

19.____

20. Workers at a juvenile detention center are responsible for establishing constructive relationships with the youths confined to the center in order to help them adjust to detention.
    Of the following, the BEST way for a worker to deal with a youth who acts over-aggressive and hostile is to
    A. take appropriate disciplinary measures
    B. attempt to distract the youth by encouraging him to engage in physical sports
    C. try to discover the real reasons for the youth's hostile behavior
    D. urge the youth to express his anger against the institution instead of *taking it out* on you

20.____

21. A worker in a men's shelter is counseling a middle-aged client for alcoholism. During counseling, the client confesses that, many years ago, he had often enjoyed sexually abusing his ten-year-old daughter. The worker tells the client that he personally finds the client's behavior *morally disgusting.*
    For the worker to tell the client this is, generally,
    A. *acceptable counseling practice*, because it may encourage the client to feel guilty about his behavior
    B. *unacceptable counseling practice*, because the client may try to shock the worker by confessing other similar behavior
    C. *acceptable counseling practice*, because *letting off steam* in this manner may relieve tension between the worker and the client
    D. *unacceptable counseling practice*, because the client may hesitate to discuss his behavior frankly with the worker in the future

21.____

22. During your discussion with a foster mother who has had a nine-year-old boy in placement for about one month, you are told that the child is disruptive in school and has been unruly and hostile toward the foster family. The boy had been quiet and docile before placement.
    In this situation, it would be MOST appropriate to suggest to the foster mother that
    A. this behavior is normal for a nine-year-old boy
    B. children placed in foster homes usually go through a period of testing their foster parents

22.____

C. the child must have picked up these patterns from the foster family
D. this behavior is probably a sign that she is too strict with the boy

23. During an interview in the housing eligibility section, your client, who wants to move to a larger apartment, asks you to decide on a suitable neighborhood for her.
For you, the worker, to make such a decision for the client would generally be considered
    A. *appropriate*, because you can save time and expense by sharing your knowledge of neighborhoods with the client
    B. *inappropriate*, because workers should not help clients with this type of decision
    C. *appropriate*, because this will help the client to develop confidence in her ability to make decisions
    D. *inappropriate*, because the client should be encouraged to accept the responsibility of making this decision

23.____

24. Your client, an elderly man left unable to care for himself after a stroke, has been referred for home-attendant services, but insists that he does not need these services. You believe that the man considers this to be an insult to his pride and that he will not allow himself to admit that he needs help.
Of the following, the MOST appropriate action for you to take is to
    A. withdraw the referral for home-attendant services and allow the client to try to take care of himself
    B. process the request for home-attendant services on the assumption that the client will soon realize that he cannot care for himself
    C. discuss with the client your interpretation of his problem and attempt to persuade him to accept home-attendant services
    D. tell the client that he will have no further opportunity to apply for home-attendant services if he does not accept them at this time

24.____

25. A worker making a field visit to investigate a complaint of child abuse finds that the parents of the child are a racially mixed couple. The child appears poorly dressed and unruly.
Of the following, the MOST appropriate approach for the worker to take in this situation is to
    A. take the child aside and ask him privately if either of his parents ever mistreats him
    B. determine if prejudice against the couple has led them to use the child as a scapegoat
    C. question the non-minority parent closely for signs of resentment of the child's mixed parentage
    D. observe the relationship between parents and child for indications of abuse by the parents

25.____

KEY (CORRECT ANSWERS)

1.	A	11.	D
2.	C	12.	A
3.	A	13.	B
4.	B	14.	B
5.	C	15.	A
6.	D	16.	B
7.	C	17.	B
8.	A	18.	B
9.	D	19.	D
10.	A	20.	C

21. D
22. B
23. D
24. C
25. D

EXAMINATION SECTION

TEST 1

DIRECTIONS: Each question or incomplete statement is followed by several suggested answers or completions. Select the one that BEST answers the question or completes the statement. *PRINT THE LETTER OF THE CORRECT ANSWER IN THE SPACE AT THE RIGHT.*

1. A client tells you that he is extremely upset by the treatment that he received from Center personnel at the information desk.
   Which of the following is the BEST way to handle this complaint during the interview?
   A. Explain to the client that he probably misinterpreted what occurred at the information desk
   B. Let the client express his feelings and then proceed with the interview
   C. Tell the client that you are not concerned with the personnel at the information desk
   D. Escort the client to the information desk to find out what really happened

   1.____

2. As a worker in the foster home division, you are reviewing a case record to determine whether a 13-year-old boy, in foster care because of neglect and mistreatment by his natural parents, should be returned home. The natural parents, who want to take the child back, have been in family counseling, with encouraging result, and have improved their living conditions.
   Of the following, it would be appropriate to recommend that the child
   A. remain with the foster parents, since this is a documented case of child abuse
   B. remain with the foster parents until they are ready to send him home
   C. be returned to his natural parents, since they have made positive efforts to change their behavior toward the child
   D. be returned to his natural parents, because continued separation will cause irreparable damage to the child

   2.____

3. You are finishing an interview with a client in which you have explained to her the procedure she must go through to apply for income maintenance.
   Of the following, the BEST way for you to make sure that she has fully understood the procedure is too ask her
   A. whether she feels she has understood your explanation of the procedure
   B. whether she has any questions to ask you about the procedure
   C. to describe the procedure to you in her own words
   D. a few questions to test her understanding of the procedure

   3.____

4. Mrs. Carey, a widow with five children, has come to the field office to seek foster care for her 13-year-old daughter, who has often been truant from school and has recently been caught shoplifting. Mrs. Carey says that she cannot maintain a proper home environment for the other four children and deal with her daughter at the same time.

   4.____

Of the following, you should FIRST
- A. process Mrs. Carey's request for placement of her daughter in a foster care agency
- B. interview both Mrs. Carey and her daughter to get a more complete picture of the situation
- C. suggest to Mrs. Care that she might be able to manage if she obtained homemaker services
- D. warn the daughter that she will be sent away from home if she does not change her behavior

5. During a group orientation meeting with couples who wish to adopt babies through your agency, one couple asks you how they should deal with the question of whether the child should be told that he is adopted.
Of the following, your BEST response to this couple is to
- A. tell them to conceal from the child the fact that he is adopted
- B. suggest that they lead the child to believe that his natural parents are dead
- C. tell them to inform the child that they know nothing about his natural parents
- D. explore with them their feelings about revealing to the child that he is adopted

6. You are beginning an investigation of an anonymous complaint that a welfare client has a concealed bank account.
Of the following, the FIRST step you should generally take in conducting this investigation is to
- A. confront the client with the complaint during an office interview
- B. try to track down the source of the anonymous complaint
- C. make a surprise visit to the client in his home to question him
- D. gather any available information from bank and agency records

7. When investigating the location of an absent parent, the worker frequently interviews the parent's friends and neighbors. The worker often writes down the information given by the person interviewed and, at the end of the interview, summarizes the information to the person.
For the worker to do this is, generally,
- A. *good practice*, because the person interviewed will be impressed by the efficiency of the worker
- B. *poor practice*, because the person interviewed may become impatient with the worker for repeating the information
- C. *good practice*, because the person interviewed has an opportunity to correct any errors the worker may have in recording the information
- D. *poor practice*, because summarizing the information may encourage the person to waste time adding and changing information

8. During an interview for the purpose of investigating a charge of child abuse, a client first denied that she had abused her child, but then burst into tears and promised that she *will never do it again*.
   Of the following, the MOST appropriate action for the worker to take in this situation is to
   A. tell the client that, since she has already lied, it is difficult to believe that she will keep her promise
   B. show a concern for the client's feelings but tell her that you will have to report your findings and refer her for help
   C. determine the extent to which the child was abused and close the case if no permanent harm was done
   D. explain to the client that she has already done enough harm to the child and you must, therefore, recommend placement

8.____

9. As a worker involved in locating absent parents, you have obtained information indicating that the address for the putative father is the same as the client's address.
   In order to determine whether, in fact, the client and putative father are living together, of the following, it would be MOST appropriate to
   A. visit the address and question the neighbors and superintendent about the putative father
   B. visit the client to ask her why she has concealed the fact that the putative father is living with her
   C. file the information in the case folder and wait for confirming information
   D. close the client's case and issue a recoupment notice to the putative father

9.____

10. A client claims that she never received a welfare check that was due her. As part of your investigation of her claim, you obtain from the bank a copy of the check, which has been endorsed with her name and cashed.
    Of the following, the BEST procedure for you to follow in this investigation is to
    A. end the investigation immediately, since the client's claim cannot be proved
    B. interview the client and show her the copy of the cashed check
    C. tell the client that you have evidence that her claim is false
    D. say nothing about the cashed check and try to trap the client in a false statement

10.____

11. As part of the investigation to locate an absent father, you make a field visit to interview one of the father's friends. Before beginning the interview, you identify yourself to the friend and show him your official identification.
    For you to do this is, generally,
    A. *good practice*, because the friend will have proof that you are authorized to make such confidential investigations
    B. *poor practice*, because the friend may not answer your questions when he knows why you are interviewing him

11.____

C. *good practice*, because your supervisor can confirm from the friend that you actually made the interview
D. *poor practice*, because the friend may warn the absent father that your agency is looking for him

12. As a field office worker you are investigating a citizen's complaint charging a mother of three children with child neglect. The mother tells you that her husband has become depressed after losing his job and is often abusive to her, and that this situation has made her feel anxious and has made it difficult for her to care for the children properly.
Which one of the following is the BEST way for you to respond to this situation?
    A. Tell the mother that she must do everything possible to help her husband find a job
    B. Arrange to meet the husband so you can explain to him the consequences of his behavior
    C. Investigate the complaint, report your findings, and refer the family for counseling or other appropriate services
    D. Suggest that the family obtain homemaker services so that the mother can go to work

13. You are interviewing a client in his home as part of your investigation of an anonymous complaint that he has been receiving Medicaid fraudulently. During the interview, the client frequently interrupts your questions to discuss the hardships of his life and the bitterness he feels about his medical condition.
Of the following, the BEST way for you to deal with these discussions is to
    A. cut them off abruptly, since the client is probably just trying to avoid answering your questions
    B. listen patiently, since these discussions may be helpful to the client and may give you information for your investigation
    C. remind the client that you are investigating a complaint against him and he must answer directly
    D. seek to gain the client's confidence by discussing any personal or medical problems which you yourself may have

14. While interviewing an absent father to determine his ability to pay child support, you realize that his answers to some of your questions contradict his answers to other questions.
Of the following, the BEST way for you to try to get accurate information from the father is to
    A. confront him with his contradictory answers and demand an explanation from him
    B. use your best judgment as to which of his answers are accurate and question him accordingly
    C. tell him that he has misunderstood your questions and that he must clarify his answers
    D. ask him the same questions in different words and follow up his answers with related questions

15. You are assigned to investigate a complaint of child neglect made against a minority mother by her non-minority neighbor. During an interview with you, the neighbor states that the mother allows her children to run around the streets half-dressed till late at night, and adds: *Of course, what can you expect from any of those people anyway?*
Your MOST appropriate action is to
   A. end the investigation, since the neighbor is clearly too prejudiced to be reliable
   B. tell the mother that the neighbor has made a complaint of child neglect against her
   C. seek evidence to support the complaint of child neglect made by the neighbor
   D. continue the interview with the neighbor in an attempt to get at the root of his prejudice against the mother

16. You are interviewing a couple with regard to available services for the husband's aged mother. During the interview, the husband casually mentions that he and his wife are thinking about becoming foster parents and would like to get some information on foster care programs offered through the Department of Social Services.
Of the following agencies within social services, the MOST appropriate one for you to refer this couple to is
   A. family and adult services
   B. special services for children
   C. bureau of child support
   D. special services for adults

17. You have been helping one of your clients to obtain medical assistance for her two young children. Accidentally, you obtain evidence that the client may be involved in a criminal scheme to collect duplicate welfare checks at several different addresses.
Of the following offices of the Department of Social Services, the MOST appropriate one to which you should report this evidence is
   A. the inspector general
   B. case intake and management
   C. the general counsel
   D. income support

Questions 18-25.

DIRECTIONS: Questions 18 through 25 are to be answered SOLELY on the basis of the Fact Situation and Report Form.

FACT SITUATION

On June 5, 2020, Mary Adams (Case No. 2095732), living at 1507 Montague Street, Apt. 3C, Brooklyn, New York, applied and was accepted for public assistance for herself and her three dependent children. Her husband, John, had left their home after an argument the previous week and had not returned, leaving Mrs. Adams without funds of any kind. She had tried to contact him at his place of employment, but was told that he had resigned several days prior to her call. When the case worker questioned Mrs. Adams about her husband's employment, income, and bank accounts, Mrs. Adams stated that he had done carpentry work during most of the years he had worked; his last known employer had been the Avco Lumber Company, 309 Amber Street, Queens, New York, where he had earned a weekly salary of $300. She then showed the case worker two bankbooks in her husband's name, which indicated a balance of $500 in one account and $275 in the other. A visit to Mr. Brown, a neighbor of the Adams', by the case worker, revealed that Mr. Adams had also told Mr. Brown about the existence of the bankbooks. A visit to the Avco Lumber Company by the case worker confirmed that Mr. Adams' gross salary had been $300 a week. This visit also revealed that Mr. Adams was a member of the Woodworkers' Union, Local #3, and that Mr. Adams' previous home address for the period February '09 to June '15 was 1109 Wellington Street, Brooklyn, New York.

REPORT FORM

A. **CLIENT**:
   1. Name:_____
   2. Address:_____
   3. Case No:_____
   4. Acceptance Date:_____
   5. No. of Dependent Children:_____

B. **ABSENT PARENT**:
   1. Name:_____
   2. Date of Birth:_____
   3. Place of Birth:_____
   4. Present Address:_____
   5. Regular Occupation:_____
   6. Union Affiliation:_____
   7. Name of Last Employer:_____
   8. Address of Last Employer:_____
   9. a. Weekly Earnings (Gross):_____
       b. How Verified:_____
   10. a. Weekly Earnings (Net):_____
       b. How Verified:_____
   11. a. Amount of Bank Accounts:_____
       b. How Verified:_____
   12. Social Security No.:_____
   13. Last Known Home Address:_____
   14. Previous Address:_____

---

18. Based on the information given in the Fact Situation, the MOST appropriate of the following entries for Item B.11.b is:
    A. Revealed to case worker by Mrs. Adams
    B. Confirmed by visit to Mr. Brown
    C. Revealed by Woodworkers' Union, Local #7
    D. Confirmed by bankbooks shown by Mrs. Adams

18.____

7 (#1)

19. The one of the following which BEST answers Item B.4 is   19.____
    A. Unknown
    B. c/o Avco Lumber Company
    C. 1109 Wellington Street, Brooklyn, New York
    D. 1507 Montague Street, Brooklyn, New York

20. Based on the information given in the Fact Situation, it is NOT possible to   20.____
    answer Item
    A. A.2   B. A.5   C. B.6   D. B.10

21. The one of the following which would be LEAST helpful in tracing the missing   21.____
    parent is information found in Item
    A. B.12   B. B.10.a C. B.6   D. B.1

22. Based on the information given in the Fact Situation, it is MOST likely that   22.____
    the same entry would be made for Items
    A. A.1 and B.1   B. A.4 and B.2
    C. B.9.a and B.10.a   D. A.2 and B.13

23. Based on the information in the Fact Situation, the entry: 1109 Wellington   23.____
    Street, Brooklyn, New York would MOST likely be placed for Item
    A. A.2   B. B.4   C. B.8   D. B.14

24. The one of the following items that can be answered based on the information   24.____
    given in the Fact Situation is
    A. B.2   B. B.3   C. B.9.b   D. B.12

25. Based on the information given in the Fact Situation, the figure 775 would   25.____
    appear in the entry for
    A. A.3   B. B.12   C. B.9.a   D. B.11.a

KEY (CORRECT ANSWERS)

1. B
2. C
3. C
4. B
5. D

6. D
7. C
8. B
9. A
10. B

11. A
12. C
13. B
14. D
15. C

16. B
17. A
18. D
19. A
20. D

21. B
22. D
23. D
24. C
25. D

TEST 2

DIRECTIONS: Each question or incomplete statement is followed by several suggested answers or completions. Select the one that BEST answers the question or completes the statement. *PRINT THE LETTER OF THE CORRECT ANSWER IN THE SPACE AT THE RIGHT.*

1. A worker in a senior adult center is approached by one of his clients, an elderly man living alone and suffering from severe arthritis, who asks him how to go about obtaining homemaker services through the Department of Social Services.
   Of the following, the MOST appropriate office of the department to which the worker should refer this client is
   A. income support
   B. protective services for adults
   C. income maintenance
   D. case intake and management

   1._____

2. Workers assigned to locate absent parents frequently ask various governmental agencies to search their records for information useful in determining the address of the person they are seeking.
   Of the following, which is likely to be useful MOST frequently for this purpose is the
   A. motor vehicle bureau
   B. office of the district attorney
   C. department of investigation
   D. health and hospitals corporation

   2._____

Questions 3-7.

DIRECTIONS: Questions 3 through 7 are to be answered SOLELY on the basis of the following Fact Situation and Preliminary Investigation Form.

FACT SITUATION

COMPLAINT:
On March 1, Mrs. Mona Willard, a neighbor of the Smith family, reported to the Police Department that the Smith children were being severely neglected, and she requested that an investigation be conducted. She based her complaint on the fact that, since the time three weeks ago when Janet Smith's husband, Charles, deserted Mrs. Smith and their two children, John, age 2, and Darlene, age 4, the children have been seen wandering in the neighborhood at all hours, inadequately dressed against the cold.

INVESTIGATION:
Investigation by the Police Department and the Department of Social Services revealed that the above charge was true and, further, that Mrs. Smith had inflicted cruel and harsh physical treatment upon the children in an attempt to discipline them. The children were immediately removed from their parent's care and placed in a medical facility for tests and observation. It was found that the children were suffering from serious malnutrition and anemia and that they also showed signs of emotional disturbance.

2 (#2)

CASE ACTION DECISION:
Conferences which you, the case worker, have held with Dr. Charles Jordan, a physician treating Mrs. Smith, and with Ellen Farraday, a psychiatric social worker from the Mental Health Consultation Center, confirm that Mrs. Smith is emotionally unstable at the present time and cannot care for her children. A written report from the Chief Resident Physician at the hospital where the children have been placed indicates that both children are presently doing well, but when released will need the security of an emotionally stable atmosphere. It has therefore been decided that placement in a foster home is necessary for the children until such time as Mrs. Smith is judged to be capable of caring for them.

PRELIMINARY INVESTIGATION FORM

1. Child(ren) in Need of Protection:
   a. Name(s):_____
   b. Age(s):_____

2. Alleged Perpetrator:
   a. Name_____
   b. Relationship_____

3. Present Status of Child(ren):
   ☐ a. Remaining with Subject Pending Investigation
   ☐ b. Removed to Relatives
   ☐ c. Removed to Foster Care
   ☐ d. In Hospital
   ☐ e. Other

4. Actions or Services Needed for Child(ren)
   ☐ a. Housekeeper
   ☐ b. Homemaker
   ☐ c. Day Care
   ☐ d. Home Attendant
   ☐ e. Relatives
   ☐ f. Foster Care

5. Contacts Made to Support Case Action Decision

	I Phone	II Personal	III Written
a. Medical; School	☐	☐	☐
b. Relatives	☐	☐	☐
c. Social Agency	☐	☐	☐
d. Other	☐	☐	☐

---

3. The one of the following that should be entered in space 2.b is   3._____
   A. mother   B. father   C. neighbor   D. physician

4. The one of the following boxes that should be checked in Item 3 is   4._____
   A. a   B. c   C. d   D. e

5. The one of the following boxes that should be checked in Item 4 is   5._____
   A. a   B. c   C. d   D. f

6. Based on the information given in the Fact Situation, the boxes that should be checked off in Item 5 are:
   A. a-II, a-III, C-II
   B. a-II, c-II, c-III
   C. a-I, a-II, a-III
   D. b-II, c-I, c-II

7. The one of the following that would CORRECTLY appear as part of the entry

Questions 8-12.

DIRECTIONS: Questions 8 through 12 are to be answered SOLELY on the basis of the information contained in the following passage.

It is desirable, whenever possible, to have long-term elderly patients return to their own homes after hospitalization, provided that the medical condition is not acute. Of course, there must be room for the patient; the family must be able to provide some necessary care; and a physician's services must be available. Although the patient's family may be able to provide most services for the patient in his own home, this is generally unlikely because of the nature of the illness and the patient's need for a variety of services. Recently, hospital personnel, public health workers, visiting nurse associations, and community leaders have been developing home-care programs, which make the services of the hospital available to the patient who is not ill enough to require the concentrated technical facilities of a general hospital, but who is unable to attend an outpatient clinic or a physician's office. These services are those of the physician, visiting nurse, physical therapist, occupational therapist, social worker, and homemaker, as needed. There is also provision for readmission to the hospital for specific purposes and return to home care.

8. According to the above passage, it would be UNDESIRABLE to have an elderly patient return to his own home after hospitalization when the patient
   A. requires the services of doctor
   B. may be in immediate danger due to his medical condition
   C. is under physical or occupational therapy
   D. cannot go to the outpatient clinic of the hospital

9. According to the above passage, the *services of the hospital* which are made available by home-care programs include those of
   A. dietitians
   B. visiting nurses
   C. public health administers
   D. community workers

10. The one of the following statements about home-care programs which is BEST supported by the above paragraph is that home-care programs
    A. have been developed in part by hospital personnel
    B. relieve workloads of hospital personnel
    C. decrease public expenditures for hospitalization of the elderly
    D. reduce readmissions of elderly patients to hospitals

11. According to the above passage, home-care programs would be LEAST likely to include the services of a
    A. homemaker
    B. social worker
    C. physician
    D. hospital technician

12. It may be inferred from the above passage that a MAJOR purpose of home-care programs is to
    A. increase the demand for physicians, nurses, and other medical personnel
    B. provide patients in their homes with services similar to those provided in hospitals
    C. reduce the need for general hospitals and outpatient clinics
    D. relieve the family of their responsibility of caring for the patient

Questions 13-17.

DIRECTIONS: Questions 13 through 17 are to be answered SOLELY on the basis of the information contained in the following Duties Statement.

DUTIES STATEMENT OF THE VIOLATION CENTER (VC) CASE WORKER

1. Receives telephone, mail, and in-person reports of suspected violations from mandated and non-mandated sources, as well as from the New York State Violation Bureau (NYSVB), on form DSS-555, within 48 hours, to the Central Office of VC, 265 Church Street, New York, N.Y.

2. Completes in-office portion of DSS-555 received from mandated sources as fully as possible. Checks that report summary is specific, factual, and detailed. (See NYSVB instructions on Page 213)

3. When DSS-555 is received, clears Central Office of VC for any previous record of violation on file in Central Office. If record exists, enters additional information from file record on to DSS-555. Also requests Central Office Clerk to provide appropriate record number of previous record and enters additional information from file record on to DSS-555. Also requests Central Office Clerk to provide appropriate record number of previous record and enters it in correct box on form.

4. Determines appropriate Central Office Sex Code and Reporting Source Code for each violation. (The Codes are in the VC Manual.) The codes are then entered on the bottom of the reverse side of the DSS-555.

5. Determines appropriate Service Area Code for the address in the summary. The address is the location of the violation, if known. (If the location of the violation is unknown, the address of the primary witness shall be used.) Enters Service Area Code on reverse of DSS-555. All report summaries involving violations by N.Y.C. employees are sent to the Manhattan Borough Office of VC for clearance and transmittal to BEM.

---

13. According to the above Duties Statement, when a report of a suspected violation is received, a written summary of their report on DSS-555 must be sent within 48 hours by
    A. mandated sources
    B. non-mandated sources
    C. the NYSVB
    D. mandated and non-mandated sources, as well as by the NYSVB

14. From the above Duties Statement, it may be *inferred* that the case worker whose duties are described is MOST likely assigned to
    A. the Manhattan Borough Office of VC
    B. the New York State Violation Bureau
    C. the Central Office of VC
    D. BEM

    14.____

15. According to the above Duties Statement, the Central Office Sex Code is entered on the DSS-555
    A. on the opposite side from the Service Area Code
    B. on the front of the form
    C. above the Service Area Code on the form
    D. on the bottom of the back of the form

    15.____

16. According to the above Duties Statement, a case worker can determine the appropriate Reporting Source Code for a violation by consulting
    A. NYSVB Instructions
    B. the Central Office Clerk
    C. the VC Manual
    D. the Service Area Code

    16.____

17. As used in paragraph 2 of the above Duties Statement, the word *detailed* means MOST NEARLY
    A. full descriptive
    B. complicated
    C. of considerable length
    D. well-written

    17.____

Questions 18-25.

DIRECTIONS: Questions 18 through 25 are to be answered SOLELY on the basis of the following Semi-Monthly Family Allowance Schedule for Maintenance of Legally Responsible Relative (Figure No. 1) and Conversion Table (Figure 2) given on the following pages and the information and case situations given below).

FIGURE NO. 1

SEMI-MONTHLY FAMILY ALLOWANCE SCHEDULE FOR MAINTENANCE OF LEGALLY RESPONSIBLE RELATIVE AND DEPENDENTS BASED UPON TOTAL NUMBER OF PERSONS IN PRESENT HOUSEHOLD. (ALL SURPLUS IS TO BE USED AS CONTRIBUTION TO RECIPIENTS OF PUBLIC ASSISTANCE.)

TOTAL NUMBER OF PERSONS IN PRESENT HOUSEHOLD	ONE	TWO	THREE	FOUR	FIVE	SIX	EACH ADDITIONAL PERSON
SEMI-MONTHLY FAMILY ALLOWANCE	$1,600	$1,915	$2,200	$2,605	$2,800	$3,205	$350

FIGURE NO. 2
CONVERSION TABLE – WEEKLY TO SEMI-MONTHLY AMOUNTS

DOLLARS				CENTS			
Weekly Amount	Semi-Monthly Amount	Weekly Amount	Semi-Monthly Amount	Weekly Amount	Semi-Monthly Amount	Weekly Amount	Semi-Monthly Amount
$10	$21.70	$510.00	$1105.00	$0.10	$0.20	$5.10	$11.10
20.00	86.70	520.00	1126.70	0.20	0.40	5.20	11.30
30.00	65.00	530.00	1148.30	0.30	0.70	5.30	11.50
40.00	86.70	540.00	1170.00	0.40	0.90	5.40	11.70
50.00	108.30	550.00	1191.70	0.50	1.10	5.50	11.90
60.00	130.00	560.00	1213.30	0.60	1.30	5.60	12.10
70.00	151.70	570.00	1235.00	0.70	1.50	5.70	12.40
80.00	173.30	580.00	1256.70	1.00	1.70	5.80	12.60
90.00	195.00	590.00	1278.30	0.90	2.00	5.90	12.80
100.00	216.70	600.00	1300.00	1.00	2.20	6.00	13.00
110.00	238.30	610.00	1321.70	1.10	2.40	6.10	13.20
120.00	260.00	620.00	1343.30	1.20	2.60	6.20	13.40
130.00	281.70	630.00	1365.00	1.30	2.80	6.30	13.70
140.00	303.30	640.00	1386.70	1.40	3.00	6.40	13.90
150.00	325.00	650.00	1408.30	1.50	3.30	6.50	14.10
160.00	346.70	660.00	1430.00	1.60	3.50	6.60	14.30
170.00	368.30	670.00	1451.40	1.70	3.70	6.70	14.50
180.00	390.00	680.00	1473.30	1.80	3.90	6.80	14.70
190.00	411.70	690.00	1495.00	1.90	4.10	6.90	15.00
200.00	433.30	700.00	1516.70	2.00	4.30	7.00	15.20
210.00	455.00	710.00	1538.30	2.10	4.60	7.10	15.40
220.00	476.70	720.00	1560.00	2.20	4.80	7.20	15.60
230.00	498.30	730.00	1581.70	2.30	5.00	7.30	15.80
240.00	520.00	740.00	1603.30	2.40	5.20	7.40	16.00
250.00	541.70	750.00	1625.00	2.50	5.40	7.50	16.30
260.00	563.30	760.00	1646.70	2.60	5.60	7.60	16.50
270.00	585.00	770.00	1668.30	2.70	5.90	7.70	16.70
280.00	606.70	780.00	690.00	2.80	6.10	7.80	16.90
290.00	628.30	790.00	1711.70	2.90	6.30	7.90	17.10
300.00	650.00	800.00	1733.30	3.00	6.50	8.00	17.30
310.00	671.70	810.00	1755.00	3.10	6.70	8.10	17.60
320.00	693.30	820.00	1776.70	3.20	6.90	8.20	17.80
330.00	715.00	830.00	1798.30	3.30	7.20	8.30	18.00
340.00	736.70	840.00	1820.00	3.40	7.40	8.40	18.20
350.00	783.00	850.00	1841.70	3.50	7.60	8.50	18.40
360.00	780.00	860.00	1863.30	3.60	7.80	8.60	18.60
370.00	801.70	870.00	1885.00	3.70	8.00	8.70	18.90
380.00	823.30	880.00	1906.70	3.80	8.20	8.80	19.10
390.00	845.00	890.00	1928.30	3.90	8.50	8.90	19.30
400.00	866.70	900.00	1950.00	4.00	8.70	9.00	19.50
410.00	888.30	910.00	1971.70	4.10	8.90	9.10	19.70
420.00	910.00	920.00	1993.30	4.20	9.10	9.20	19.90
430.00	931.70	930.00	2015.00	4.30	9.30	9.30	20.20
440.00	953.30	940.00	2036.70	40.40	9.50	9.40	20.40
450.00	975.00	950.00	2058.30	40.50	9.80	9.50	20.60
460.00	996.70	960.00	2080.00	4.60	10.00	9.60	20.80
470.00	1018.30	970.00	2101.70	4.70	10.20	9.70	21.00
480.00	1040.00	980.00	2123.30	4.80	10.40	9.80	21.20
490.00	1061.70	990.00	2145.00	4.90	10.60	9.90	21.50
500.00	1083.30	1000.00	2166.70	5.00	10.80		

INFORMATION

Legally responsible relatives living apart from persons on public assistance are asked to contribute toward the support of these persons. The amount of contribution depends on several factors, such as the number of persons in the legally responsible relative's present household who are dependent on his income (including himself), the amount of his gross income, and his expenses incident to employment. Since his contribution is computed on a semi-monthly basis, all figures must be broken down into semi-monthly amounts. Weekly amounts can be converted into semi-monthly amounts by using the conversion table on page 6.

The amount of supported is computed as follows:

1. Determine total weekly gross income (the wages or salary before payroll deductions) of legally responsible relative.
2. Deduct all weekly expenses incident to employment such as federal, state, and city income taxes, Social Security payments, State Disability Insurance payments, union dues, cost of transportation, and $10.00 maximum per work day for lunch.
3. Remaining income shall be considered as weekly net income of legally responsible relative.
4. Convert weekly net income to semi-monthly net income, using data in Figure No. 2.
5. Semi-monthly net income is compared to the semi-monthly allowance (see Figure No. 1). If there is an excess of net income, then that amount is considered available as the contribution to the public assistance household. If the semi-monthly allowance is greater than the semi-monthly net income, then there is an income deficit, and there is no income available as a contribution to the public assistance household.
6. The formula for computing the semi-monthly contribution is:
Semi-Monthly Net Income • Semi-Monthly Family Allowance = Semi-Monthly Amount of Income Available Towards Contribution to Public Assistance Household

Case Situation No. 1:

Mr. Andrew Young is separated from his wife and family and lives with one dependent in a 3-room furnished apartment. Mr. Young is employed as a dishwasher and his gross wages are $1,000 per week. He is employed 5 days a week and spends $14.40 a day for carfare. He spends $20.00 a work day on lunch. His weekly salary deductions are as follows:

Federal Income Tax	$142.30
State Income Tax	26.00
City Income Tax	9.80
Social Security	62.10
New York State Disability Insurance	5.30
Union Due	5.00

Mr. Young's wife and two children, for whom he is legally responsible, are currently receiving public assistance.

8 (#2)

18. The weekly amount that Mr. Young contributes toward Social Security, New York State Disability Insurance, Income Taxes, and Union Dues is MOST NEARLY
    A. $214.70   B. $250.50   C. $320.50   D. $370.50

    18._____

19. The total amount of all weekly expenses incident to Mr. Young's employment which should be deducted from his weekly gross earnings is MOST NEARLY
    A. $214.70   B. $250.50   C. $370.50   D. $420.50

    19._____

20. Which one of the following amounts is Mr. Young's semi-monthly net income?
    A. $1259.00   B. $1363.90   C. $1623.90   D. $1701.50

    20._____

21. The semi-monthly amount of income available to the contribution to Mr. Young's wife and two children is MOST NEARLY
    A. $0.00   B. $23.90   C. $236.10   D. $551.10

    21._____

Case Situation No. 2:
Mr. Donald Wilson resides with six dependents in a seven-room unfurnished apartment. Mr. Wilson is employed as an automobile salesman and his gross wages are $4,000 per week. He is employed five days a week and spends $10.00 a day carfare. He spends $50.00 a work day for lunch. His weekly salary deductions are as follows:

Federal Income Tax	$$705.50
State Income Tax	150.00
City Income Tax	97.00
Social Security	301.00
New York State Disability Insurance	52.50
Union Due	Not Union Member

22. The weekly amount that Mr. Wilson contributes toward Social Security, New York State Disability Insurance, Federal Income Tax, and Union Dues is MOST NEARLY
    A. $1059.00   B. $1159.00   C. $1306.00   D. $1406.00

    22._____

23. The total amount of all weekly expenses incident to Mr. Wilson's employment, which should be deducted from his weekly gross earnings is MOST NEARLY
    A. $1159.00   B. $1306.00   C. $1406.00   D. $1606.00

    23._____

24. The semi-monthly family allowance for Mr. Wilson and his six dependents is MOST NEARLY
    A. $2594.00   B. $3205.00   C. $1406.00   D. $4000.00

    24._____

25. The semi-monthly amount Mr. Wilson's income available for contribution to his wife and child is MOST NEARLY
    A. $1633.00   B. $2065.40   C. $2594.00   D. $2810.20

    25._____

KEY (CORRECT ANSWERS)

1.	D	11.	D
2.	A	12.	B
3.	A	13.	A
4.	C	14.	C
5.	D	15.	D
6.	A	16.	C
7.	C	17.	A
8.	B	18.	B
9.	B	19.	C
10.	A	20.	B
21.	A		
22.	A		
23.	C		
24.	C		
25.	B		

INTERVIEWING
EXAMINATION SECTION
TEST 1

DIRECTIONS: Each question or incomplete statement is followed by several suggested answers or completions. Select the one that BEST answers the question or completes the statement. *PRINT THE LETTER OF THE CORRECT ANSWER IN THE SPACE AT THE RIGHT.*

1. You are conducting an interview with a client who has been having some difficulties with one of her fellow-workers. The client walks on crutches. You tell the client that she probably finds it difficult to get along with her fellow-workers because of this handicap.
   To make such a statement would, *generally,* be

   A. *proper;* people are often prejudiced against persons with physical deformities
   B. *proper;* statements such as this indicate to the client that you are sympathetic toward her
   C. *improper;* this approach would not help the client solve her problem
   D. *improper;* you should have discussed this handicap in relation to the client's continued ability to continue in her job

2. The information which the interviewer plans to secure from an individual with whom he talks is determined MAINLY by the

   A. purpose of the interview and the functions of the agency
   B. state assistance laws and the desires of the individual
   C. privacy they have while talking and the willingness of the individual to give information
   D. emotional feelings of the individual seeking help and the interviewer's reactions to these feelings

3. *Generally,* the MOST effective of the following ways of dealing with a person being interviewed who frequently digresses from the subject under discussion or starts to ramble, is for the interviewer to

   A. tell the person that he, the interviewer, will have to terminate the interview unless the former sticks to the point
   B. increase the tempo of the interview
   C. demonstrate that he is a good listener and allow the person to continue in his own way
   D. inject questions which relate to the purpose of the interview

4. "Being a good listener" is an interviewing technique which, if applied properly, is *desirable* MOSTLY because it

   A. catches the client more easily in misrepresentations and lies
   B. conserves the energies of the interviewer
   C. encourages the client to talk about his personal affairs without restraint
   D. encourages the giving of information which is generally more reliable and complete

5. When questioning applicants for eligibility, it would be BEST to ask questions that are

A. *direct,* so that the applicant will realize that the interviewer knows what he is doing
B. *direct,* so that the information received will be as pertinent as possible
C. *indirect,* so that the applicant will not realize the purpose of the interview
D. *indirect,* so that you can trap the applicant into making admissions that he would not otherwise make

6. The CHIEF reason for conducting an interview with a new applicant in complete privacy is that the

   A. interviewer will be better able to record the facts without any other worker reading his case notes
   B. applicant will be impressed by the business-like atmosphere of the agency
   C. interviewer will be able to devote more time to questioning the applicant without interruption
   D. applicant will be more likely to speak frankly

7. When conducting an interview with a client who is upset because of an increase in rent, it would be BEST for the interviewer to

   A. agree with the client that the agency was wrong in raising his rent, as a basis for further discussion
   B. tell the client that unless he calms down the interview will be ended
   C. prevent the client from becoming emotional
   D. tell the client the reasons for the increase

8. At an interview to determine whether an applicant is eligible, the applicant gives information different from that which he submitted on his application.
The MOST advisable action to take is to

   A. cross out the old information, enter the new information, and initial the entry
   B. re-enter the old information on the application form and initial the entry
   C. give the applicant another application form, have him fill it out correctly, and resume the interview
   D. give the applicant another application form to fill out, and set a later date for another interview

9. After you have secured, in an interview, all the necessary information from an applicant, he shows no intention of leaving, but starts to tell you a long personal story.
Of the following, the MOST advisable action for you to take is to

   A. explain to the applicant why personal stories are out of place in a business office
   B. listen carefully to the story for whatever relevant information it may contain
   C. interrupt him tactfully, thank him for the information he has already given, and terminate the interview
   D. inform your supervisor that the time required for this interview will prevent you from completing the interviews scheduled for the day

10. In interviewing, the practice of anticipating an applicant's answers to questions is, *generally,*

    A. *desirable* because it is effective and economical when it is necessary to interview large numbers of applicants
    B. *desirable* because many applicants have language difficulties

C. *undesirable* because it is the inalienable right of every person to answer as he sees fit
D. *undesirable* because applicants may tend to agree with the answer proposed by the interviewer even when the answer is not entirely correct

11. A follow-up interview was arranged for an applicant in order that he might furnish certain requested evidence. At this follow-up interview, the applicant still fails to furnish the necessary evidence.
It would be MOST advisable for you to

   A. advise the applicant that he is now considered ineligible
   B. ask the applicant how soon he can get the necessary evidence and set a date for another interview
   C. question the applicant carefully and thoroughly to determine if he has misrepresented or falsified any information
   D. set a date for another interview and tell the applicant to get the necessary evidence by that time

12. When an initial interview is being conducted, one way of starting is to explain the purpose of the interview to the applicant.
The practice of starting the interview with such an explanation is, *generally*,

   A. *desirable* because the applicant can then understand why the interview is necessary and what will be accomplished by it
   B. *desirable* because it creates the rapport which is necessary to successful interviewing
   C. *undesirable* because time will be saved by starting off directly with the questions which must be asked
   D. *undesirable* because the interviewer should have the choice of starting an interview in any manner he prefers

13. Empathy can be defined as the ability of one individual to respond sensitively and imaginatively to another's feelings.
For an interviewer to be empathic during an interview is *usually*

   A. *undesirable*, mainly because an interviewer should never be influenced by the feelings of the one being interviewed
   B. *desirable*, mainly because an interview will not be productive unless the interviewer takes the side of the person interviewed
   C. *undesirable*, mainly because empathy usually leads an interviewer to be biased in favor of the person being interviewed
   D. *desirable*, mainly because this ability allows the interviewer to direct his questions more effectively to the person interviewed

14. Assume that you must interview several people who know each other.
To gather them all in one group and question them TOGETHER, is, *generally*,

   A. *good practice*, since any inaccurate information offered by one person would be corrected by others in the group
   B. *poor practice*, since people in a group rarely pay adequate attention to questions
   C. *good practice*, since the interviewer will save much time and effort in this way
   D. *poor practice*, since the presence of several people can inhibit an individual from speaking

15. An effective interviewer should know that the one of the following reasons which LEAST describes why there is a wide range of individual behavior in human relations is that

    A. socio-economic status influences human behavior
    B. physical characteristics do not influence human behavior
    C. education influences human behavior
    D. childhood experience influences human behavior

16. An interviewer encounters an uncooperative interviewee. Of the following, the FIRST thing the interviewer should do in such a situation is to

    A. try various appeals to win the interviewee over to a cooperative attitude
    B. try to ascertain the reason for non-cooperation
    C. promise the interviewee that all data will be kept confidential
    D. alter his interviewing technique with the uncooperative interviewee

17. You discover that an interviewee who was requested to bring with him specific documents for his initial employment interview has forgotten the documents.
    Of the following, the BEST course of action to take is to

    A. give the person a reasonable amount of time to furnish the documents
    B. tell the person you will let him know how much additional time he has
    C. mark the person disqualified for employment; he has failed to provide reasonably requested data on time
    D. mark the person provisionally qualified for employment; upon receipt of the documents he will be permanently qualified

18. In checking interviewees' work experience, you realize that the person whom you are to interview is only marginally fluent in English and has, therefore, requested permission to bring a translator with him.
    Of the following, the BEST course of action is to inform the interviewee that

    A. outside translators may not be used
    B. only city translators may be used
    C. state law requires fluency in English of all civil servants
    D. he may be assisted in the interview by his translator

19. Assume that, during the course of an interview, you are verbally attacked by the person being interviewed.
    Of the following, it would be MOST advisable to

    A. answer back in a matter-of-fact manner
    B. ask the person to apologize and discontinue the interview
    C. ignore the attack but adjourn the interview to another day
    D. use restraint and continue the interview

20. Assume that you find that the person you are interviewing has difficulty finishing his sentences and seems to be groping for words.
    In such a case, the BEST approach for you to take is to

    A. say what you think the person has in mind
    B. proceed patiently without calling attention to the problem
    C. ask the person why he finds it difficult to finish his sentences
    D. interrupt the interview until the person feels more relaxed

21. The one of the following which BEST describes the effect of the *sympathetic approach* in interviewing on the interviewee is that it will 21.____

    A. have no discernible effect on the interviewee
    B. calm the interviewee
    C. lead the interviewee to underemphasize his problems
    D. mislead the interviewee

22. The one of the following characteristics which is a PRIMARY requisite for a successful interview is 22.____

    A. total *curiosity*
    B. total *sympathy*
    C. complete *attention*
    D. complete *dedication*

23. Assume that you have been assigned to conduct a follow-up interview with a primary witness. 23.____
    The one of the following which is MOST important in arranging such an interview is to

    A. keep the witness cooperative
    B. conduct the matter in secret
    C. allow the witness to determine where and when the interview takes place
    D. conduct the interview as soon as possible to insure a strong case

24. By examining a candidate's employment record, an interviewer can determine many things about the candidate. Of the following, the one which is LEAST apparent from an employment record is the candidate's 24.____

    A. character
    B. willingness to work
    C. capacity to get along with co-workers
    D. potential for advancing in civil service

25. Assume that you are conducting an interview in which the person being interviewed is using the interview as a forum for venting his anti-civil service feelings. 25.____
    Of the following, the FIRST thing that you should do is to

    A. agree with the person; perhaps that will shorten the outburst
    B. respectfully disagree with the person; the decorum of the interview has already been disrupted
    C. courteously and objectively direct the interview to the relevant issue
    D. reschedule the interview to another mutually agreeable time

KEY (CORRECT ANSWERS)

1. C
2. A
3. D
4. D
5. B

6. D
7. D
8. A
9. C
10. D

11. B
12. A
13. D
14. D
15. B

16. B
17. A
18. D
19. D
20. B

21. C
22. C
23. A
24. D
25. C

TEST 2

DIRECTIONS: Each question or incomplete statement is followed by several suggested answers or completions. Select the one that BEST answers the question or completes the statement. *PRINT THE LETTER OF THE CORRECT ANSWER IN THE SPACE AT THE RIGHT.*

1. The pattern of an interview is LARGELY set by the 1._____

   A. person being interviewed
   B. person conducting the interview
   C. nature of the interview
   D. policy of the agency employing the interviewer

2. Assume that a person being interviewed, who had been talking freely, suddenly tries to change the subject. 2._____
   To a trained interviewer, this behavior would mean that the person *probably*

   A. knew very little about the subject
   B. realized that he was telling too much
   C. decided that his privacy was being violated
   D. realized that he was becoming confused

3. Assume that you receive a telephone call from an unknown individual requesting information about a person you are currently interviewing. 3._____
   In such a situation, the BEST course of action for you to take is to

   A. give him the information over the telephone
   B. tell him to write to your department for the information
   C. send him the information, retaining a copy for your files
   D. tell him to call back, giving you additional time to check into the matter

4. In an interview, assuming that the interviewer was using a *non-directive approach* in this interview, of the following, the interviewer's most effective response would be: 4._____

   A. "You know, you are building a bad record of tardiness."
   B. "Can you tell me more about this situation?"
   C. "What kind of person is your superior?"
   D. "Do you think you are acting fairly towards the agency by being late so often?"

5. In an interview, assuming that the interviewer was using a *directed approach* in this interview, of the following, the interviewer's response should be: 5._____

   A. "That doesn't seem like much of an excuse to me."
   B. "What do you mean by saying that you've lost interest?"
   C. "What problems are there with the supervision you are getting?"
   D. "How do you think your tardiness looks in your personnel record?"

Questions 6-8.

DIRECTIONS: Answer Questions 6 through 8 only on the basis of information given in the passage below.

A personnel interviewer, selecting job applicants, may find that he reacts badly to some people even on first contact. This reaction cannot usually be explained by things that the interviewee has done or said. Most of us have had the experience of liking or disliking, of feeling comfortable or uncomfortable with people on first acquaintance, long before we have had a chance to make a conscious, rational decision about them. Often, too, our liking or disliking is transmitted to the other person by subtle processes such as gestures, posture, voice intonations, or choice of words. The point to be kept in mind in this: the relations between people are complex and occur at several levels, from the conscious to the unconscious. This is true whether the relationship is brief or long, formal or informal.

Some of the major dynamics of personality which operate on the unconscious level are projection, sublimation, rationalization, and repression. Encountering these for the first time, one is apt to think of them as representing pathological states. In the extreme, they undoubtedly are, but they exist so universally that we must consider them also to be parts of normal personality.

Without necessarily subscribing to any of the numerous theories of personality, it is possible to describe personality in terms of certain important aspects or elements. We are all aware of ourselves as thinking organisms.

This aspect of personality, the conscious part, is important for understanding human behavior, but it is not enough. Many find it hard to accept the notion that each person also has an unconscious. The existence of the unconscious is no longer a matter of debate. It is not possible to estimate at all precisely what proportion of our total psychological life is conscious, what proportion unconscious. Everyone who has studied the problem, however, agrees that consciousness is the smaller part of personality. Most of what we are and do is a result of unconscious processes. To ignore this is to risk mistakes.

6. The passage above suggests that an interviewer can be MOST effective if he

   A. learns how to determine other peoples' unconscious motivations
   B. learns how to repress his own unconsciously motivated mannerisms and behavior
   C. can keep others from feeling that he either likes or dislikes them
   D. gains an understanding of how the unconscious operates in himself and in others

7. It may be inferred from the passage above that the "subtle processes, such as gestures, posture, voice intonation, or choice of words," referred to in the first paragraph, are, *usually,*

   A. in the complete control of an expert interviewer
   B. the determining factors in the friendships a person establishes
   C. controlled by a person's unconscious
   D. not capable of being consciously controlled

8. The passage above implies that various different personality theories are, *usually,*

   A. so numerous and different as to be valueless to an interviewer
   B. in basic agreement about the importance of the unconscious
   C. understood by the interviewer who strives to be effective
   D. in agreement that personality factors such as projection and repression are pathological

Questions 9-10.

DIRECTIONS: Answer Questions 9 and 10 ONLY on the basis of information given in the passage below.

   Since we generally assure informants that what they say is confidential, we are not free to tell one informant what the other has told us. Even if the informant says, "I don't care who knows it; tell anybody you want to," we find it wise to treat the interview as confidential. An interviewer who relates to some informants what other informants have told him is likely to stir up anxiety and suspicion. Of course, the interviewer may be able to tell an informant what he has heard without revealing the source of his information. This may be perfectly appropriate where a story has wide currency so that an informant cannot infer the source of the information. But if an event is not widely known, the mere mention of it may reveal to one informant what another informant has said about the situation. How can the data be cross-checked in these circumstances?

9. The passage above implies that the anxiety and suspicion an interviewer may arouse by telling what has been learned in other interviews is due to the

   A. lack of trust the person interviewed may have in the interviewer's honesty
   B. troublesome nature of the material which the interviewer has learned in other interviews
   C. fact that the person interviewed may not believe that permission was given to repeat the information
   D. fear of the person interviewed that what he is telling the interviewer will be repeated

9._____

10. The paragraph above is *most likely* part of a longer passage dealing with

    A. ways to verify data gathered in interviews
    B. the various anxieties a person being interviewed may feel
    C. the notion that people sometimes say things they do not mean
    D. ways an interviewer can avoid seeming suspicious

10._____

Questions 11-12.

DIRECTIONS: Answer Questions 11 and 12 ONLY on the basis of information given below.

   The ability to interview rests not only on any single trait, but on a vast complex of them. Habits, skills, techniques, and attitudes are all involved. Competence in interviewing is acquired only after careful and diligent study, prolonged practice (preferably under supervision), and a good bit of trial and error; for interviewing is not an exact science, it is an art. Like many other arts, however, it can and must draw on science in several of its aspects.

   There is always a place for individual initiative, for imaginative innovations, and for new combinations of old approaches. The skilled interviewer cannot be bound by a set of rules. Likewise, there is not a set of rules which can guarantee to the novice that his interviewing will be successful. There are, however, some accepted, general guide-posts which may help the beginner to avoid mistakes, learn how to conserve his efforts, and establish effective working relationships with interviewees; to accomplish, in short, what he set out to do.

11. According to the passage above, rules and standard techniques for interviewing are

11._____

4 (#2)

- A. helpful for the beginner, but useless for the experienced, innovative interviewer
- B. destructive of the innovation and initiative needed for a good interviewer
- C. useful for even the experienced interviewer, who may, however, sometimes go beyond them
- D. the means by which nearly anybody can become an effective interviewer

12. According to the passage above, the one of the following which is a prerequisite to competent interviewing is 12.____

    - A. avoiding mistakes
    - B. study and practice
    - C. imaginative innovation
    - D. natural aptitude

Questions 13-16.

DIRECTIONS: Answer Questions 13 through 16 SOLELY on the basis of information given in the following paragraph.

The question of what material is relevant is not as simple as it might seem. Frequently material which seems irrelevant to the inexperienced has, because of the common tendency to disguise and distort and misplace one's feelings, considerable significance. It may be necessary to let the client "ramble on" for a while in order to clear the decks, as it were, so that he may get down to things that really are on his mind. On the other hand, with an already disturbed person, it may be important for the interviewer to know when to discourage further elaboration of upsetting material. This is especially the case where the worker would be unable to do anything about it. An inexperienced interviewer might, for instance, be intrigued with the bizarre elaboration of material that the psychotic produces, but further elaboration of this might encourage the client in his instability. A too random discussion may indicate that the interviewee is not certain in what areas the interviewer is prepared to help him, and he may be seeking some direction. Or again, satisfying though it may be for the interviewer to have the interviewee tell him intimate details, such revelations sometimes need to be checked or encouraged only in small doses. An interviewee who has "talked too much" often reveals subsequent anxiety. This is illustrated by the fact that? frequently after a "confessional" interview ,the interviewee surprises the interviewer by being withdrawn, inarticulate, or hostile, or by breaking the next appointment.

13. Sometimes a client may reveal certain personal information to an interviewer and subsequently, may feel anxious about this revelation. 13.____
    If, during an interview, a client begins to discuss very personal matters, it would be BEST to

    - A. tell the client, in no uncertain terms, that you're not interested in personal details
    - B. ignore the client at this point
    - C. encourage the client to elaborate further on the details
    - D. inform the client that the information seems to be very personal

14. Clients with severe psychological disturbances pose an especially difficult problem for the inexperienced interviewer.
The difficulty lies in the possibility of the client's

    A. becoming physically violent and harming the interviewer
    B. "rambling on" for a while
    C. revealing irrelevant details which may be followed by cancelled appointments
    D. reverting to an unstable state as a result of interview material

14.____

15. An interviewer should be constantly alert to the possibility of obtaining clues from the client as to problem areas.
According to the above passage, a client who discusses topics at random may be

    A. unsure of what problems the interviewer can provide help
    B. reluctant to discuss intimate details
    C. trying to impress the interviewer with his knowledge
    D. deciding what relevant material to elaborate on

15.____

16. The evaluation of a client's responses may reveal substantial information that may aid the interviewer in assessing the problem areas that are of concern to the client. Responses that seemed irrelevant at the time of the interview may be of significance because

    A. considerable significance is attached to all irrelevant material
    B. emotional feelings are frequently masked
    C. an initial "rambling on" is often a prelude to what -is actually bothering the client
    D. disturbed clients often reveal subsequent anxiety

16.____

Questions 17-19.

DIRECTIONS: Answer Questions 17 through 19 SOLELY on the basis of the following paragraph.

The physical setting of the interview may determine its entire potentiality. Some degree of privacy and a comfortable relaxed atmosphere are important. The interviewee is not encouraged to give much more than his name and address if the interviewer seems busy with other things, if people are rushing about, if there are distracting noises. He has a right to feel that, whether the interview lasts five minutes or an hour, he has, for that time, the undivided attention of the interviewer. Interruptions, telephone calls, and so on, should be reduced to a minimum. If the interviewee has waited in a crowded room for what seems to him an interminably long period, he is naturally in no mood to sit down and discuss what is on his mind. Indeed, by that time the primary thing on his mind may be his irritation at being kept waiting, and he frequently feels it would be impolite to express this. If a wait or interruptions have been unavoidable, it is always helpful to give the client some recognition that these are disturbing and that he can naturally understand that they make it more difficult for him to proceed. At the same time if he protests that they have not troubled him, the interviewer can best accept his statements at their face value, as further insistence that they must have been disturbing may be interpreted by him as accusing, and he may conclude that the interviewer has been personally hurt by his irritation.

17. Distraction during an interview may tend to limit the client's responses. 17.____
In a case where an interruption has occurred, it would be BEST for the interviewer to

   A. terminate this interview and have it rescheduled for another time period
   B. ignore the interruption since it is not continuous
   C. express his understanding that the distraction can cause the client to feel disturbed
   D. accept the client's protests that he has been troubled by the interruption

18. To maximize the rapport that can be established with the client, an appropriate physical 18.____
setting is necessary. At the very least, some privacy would be necessary.
In addition, the interviewer should

   A. always appear to be busy in order to impress the client
   B. focus his attention only on the client
   C. accept all the client's statements as being valid
   D. stress the importance of the interview to the client

19. Clients who have been waiting quite some time for their interview may, justifiably, become 19.____
upset. However, a client *may initially* attempt to mask these feelings because he may

   A. personally hurt the interviewer
   B. want to be civil
   C. feel that the wait was unavoidable
   D. fear the consequences of his statement

20. You have been assigned to interview W, a witness, concerning a minor automobile acci- 20.____
dent. Although you have made no breach of the basic rules of contact and approach,
you, nevertheless, recognize that you and W have a personality clash and that a natural
animosity has resulted.
Of the following, you MOST appropriately should

   A. discuss the personality problem with W and attempt to resolve the difference
   B. stop the interview on some pretext and leave in a calm and pleasant manner, allowing an associate to continue the interview
   C. ignore the personality problem and continue as though nothing had happened
   D. change the subject matter being discussed since the facts sought may be the source of the animosity

21. Assume that you desire to interview W, a reluctant witness to an event that took place 21.____
several weeks previously. Assume further that the interview can take place at a location
to be designated by the interviewer.
Of the following, the place of interview should *preferably* be the

   A. office of the interviewer
   B. home of W
   C. office of W
   D. scene where the event took place

22. Assume that you are interviewing W, a witness. During the interview it becomes apparent 22.____
that W's statements are inaccurate and at variance with the facts previously established.
In these circumstances, it would be BEST for you to

   A. tell W that his statements are inaccurate and point out how they conflict with previously established facts

B. reword your questions and ask additional questions about the facts being discussed
C. warn W that he may be required to testify under oath at a later date
D. ignore W's statements if you have other information that support the facts

23. Assume that W, a witness being interviewed by you, shows a tendency to ramble. His answers to your questions are lengthy and not responsive.
In this situation, the BEST action for you to take is to

    A. permit W to continue because at some point he will tell you the information sought
    B. tell W that he is rambling and unresponsive and that more will be accomplished if he is brief and to the point
    C. control the interview so that complete and accurate information is obtained
    D. patiently listen to W since rambling is W's style and it cannot be changed

24. Assume that you are interviewing a client. Of the following, the BEST procedure for you to follow in regard to the use of your notebook is to

    A. take out your notebook at the start of the interview and immediately begin taking notes
    B. memorize the important facts related during the interview and enter them after the interview has been completed
    C. advise the client that all his answers are being taken down to insure that he will tell the truth
    D. establish rapport with the client and ask permission to jot down various data in your notebook

25. In order to conduct an effective interview, an interviewer's attention must continuously be directed in two ways, toward himself as well as toward the interviewee. Of the following, the PRIMARY danger in this division of attention is that the

    A. interviewer's behavior may become less natural and thus alienate the interviewee
    B. interviewee's span of attention will be shortened
    C. interviewer's response may be interpreted by the interviewee as being antagonistic
    D. interviewee's more or less concealed prejudices will come to the surface

KEY (CORRECT ANSWERS)

1. B
2. B
3. B
4. B
5. C

6. D
7. C
8. B
9. D
10. A

11. C
12. B
13. D
14. D
15. A

16. B
17. C
18. B
19. B
20. B

21. A
22. B
23. C
24. D
25. A

READING COMPREHENSION
UNDERSTANDING AND INTERPRETING WRITTEN MATERIAL

EXAMINATION SECTION
TEST 1

DIRECTIONS: Each question or incomplete statement is followed by several suggested answers or completions. Select the one that BEST answers the question or completes the statement. *PRINT THE LETTER OF THE CORRECT ANSWER IN THE SPACE AT THE RIGHT.*

Questions 1-2.

DIRECTIONS: Questions 1 and 2 are to be answered SOLELY on the basis of the following passage.

   The new suburbia that is currently being built does not look much different from the old; there has, however, been an increase in the class and race polarization that has been developing between the suburbs and the cities for several generations now. The suburbs have become the home for an ever larger proportion of working-class, middle-class, and upper-class whites; the cities, for an even larger proportion of poor and non-white people. A great number of cities are 30 to 50 percent non-white in population, with more and larger ghettos than cities have ever had. Now, there is greater urban poverty on the one hand, and stronger suburban opposition to open housing and related policies to solve the cities' problems on the other hand. The urban crisis will worsen; and although there is no shortage of rational solutions, nothing much will be done about the crisis unless white America permits a radical change of public policy and undergoes a miraculous change of attitude towards its cities and their populations.

1. Which of the following statements is IMPLIED by the above passage?

    A. The percentage of non-whites in the suburbs is increasing.
    B. The policies of suburbanites have contributed to the seriousness of the urban crisis.
    C. The problems of the cities defy rational solutions.
    D. There has been a radical change in the appearance of both suburbia and the cities in the past few years.

2. Of the following, the title which BEST describes the passage's main theme is:

    A. THE NEW SUBURBIA
    B. URBAN POVERTY
    C. URBAN-SUBURBAN POLARIZATION
    D. WHY AMERICANS WANT TO LIVE IN THE SUBURBS

Questions 3-4.

DIRECTIONS: Questions 3 and 4 are to be answered selecting the BEST interpretation of the following paragraph.

One of the most familiar *type* dichotomies is Jung's introvert versus extrovert. Introverts are motivated by principles, extroverts by expediency; introverts are thinkers, extroverts are doers; and so on. Analysis of the way people react to principle versus expediency situations, however, has demonstrated that most people would have to be described as ambiverts (i.e., they exhibit both introverted and extroverted behavior depending upon the specific situation). Of course, some people behave in a more introverted way than others. A graphic representation of the number of persons exhibiting various degrees of such behavior along a continuum would approximate the familiar bell-shaped curve.

3. A. Extreme extroverts exhibit deviant behavior.
   B. The bell-shaped curve would indicate that there are slightly more introverts than extroverts.
   C. A continuum is used to determine whether a person is an introvert or an extrovert.
   D. There is really very little difference between an introvert, an extrovert, or an ambivert.

4. A. Extroverts are not thinkers, and introverts are not doers.
   B. Ambiverts *think* more than they *do*.
   C. Ambiverts outnumber introverts in the general society.
   D. Extroverts possess fewer principles than introverts.

5. The fundamental desires for food, shelter, family, and approval, and their accompanying instinctive forms of behavior, are among the most important forces in human life because they are essential to and directly connected with the preservation and the welfare of the individual as well as of the race.
   According to this statement,

   A. as long as human beings are permitted to act instinctively, they will act wisely
   B. the instinct for self-preservation makes the individual consider his own welfare rather than that of others
   C. racial and individual welfare depend upon the fundamental desires
   D. the preservation of the race demands that instinctive behavior be modified

6. The growth of our cities, the increasing tendency to move from one part of the country to another, the existence of people of different cultures in the neighborhood, have together made it more and more difficult to secure group recreation as part of informal family and neighborhood life.
   According to this statement,

   A. the breaking up of family and neighborhood ties discourages new family and neighborhood group recreation
   B. neighborhood recreation no longer forms a significant part of the larger community
   C. the growth of cities crowds out the development of all recreational activities
   D. the non-English-speaking people do not accept new activities easily

7. Sublimation consists in directing some inner urge, arising from a lower psychological level into some channel of interest on a higher psychological level. Pugnaciousness, for example, is directed into some athletic activity involving combat, such as football or boxing, where rules of fair play and the ethics of the game lift the destructive urge for combat into a constructive experience and offer opportunities for the development of character and personality.

According to this statement,

A. the manner of self-expression may be directed into constructive activities
B. athletic activities such as football and boxing are destructive of character
C. all conscious behavior on high psychological levels indicates the process of sublimation
D. the rules of fair play are inconsistent with pugnaciousness

Questions 8-9.

DIRECTIONS: Questions 8 and 9 are to be answered on the basis of the following passage.

Just why some individuals choose one way of adjusting to their difficulties and others choose other ways is not known. Yet what an individual does when he is thwarted remains a reasonably good key to the understanding of his personality. If his responses to thwart-ings are emotional explosions and irrational excuses, he is tending to live in an unreal world. He may need help to regain the world of reality, the cause-and-effect world recognized by generations of thinkers and scientists. Perhaps he needs encouragement to redouble his efforts. Perhaps, on the other hand, he is striving for the impossible and needs to substitute a worthwhile activity within the range of his abilities. It is the part of wisdom to learn the nature of the world and of oneself in relation to it and to meet each situation as intelligently and as adequately as one can.

8. The title that BEST expresses the idea of this paragraph is

   A. ADJUSTING TO LIFE
   B. ESCAPE FROM REALITY
   C. THE IMPORTANCE OF PERSONALITY
   D. EMOTIONAL CONTROL

9. The writer argues that all should

   A. substitute new activities for old
   B. redouble their efforts
   C. analyze their relation to the world
   D. seek encouragement from others

Questions 10-15.

DIRECTIONS: Questions 10 through 15 are to be answered SOLELY on the basis of the information given in the paragraph below.

The use of role-playing as a training technique was developed during the past decade by social scientists, particularly psychologists, who have been active in training experiments. Originally, this technique was applied by clinical psychologists who discovered that a patient appears to gain understanding of an emotionally disturbing situation when encouraged to act out roles in that situation. As applied in government and business organizations, the purpose of role-playing is to aid employees to understand certain work problems involving interpersonal relations and to enable observers to evaluate various reactions to them. Thus, for example, on the problem of handling grievances, two individuals from the group might be selected to act out extemporaneously the parts of subordinate and supervisor. When this situation is enacted by various pairs among the class and the techniques and results are discussed, the members of the group are presumed to reach conclusions about the most effective means of handling similar situations. Often the use of role reversal, where participants take parts different from their actual work roles, assists individuals to gain more insight into other people's problems and viewpoints. Although role-playing can be a rewarding training device, the trainer must be aware of his responsibilities. If this technique is to be successful, thorough briefing of both actors and observers as to the situation in question, the participants' roles, and what to look for, is essential.

10. The role-playing technique was FIRST used for the purpose of

    A. measuring the effectiveness of training programs
    B. training supervisors in business organizations
    C. treating emotionally disturbed patients
    D. handling employee grievances

11. When role-playing is used in private business as a training device, the CHIEF aim is to

    A. develop better relations between supervisor and subordinate in the handling of grievances
    B. come up with a solution to a specific problem that has arisen
    C. determine the training needs of the group
    D. increase employee understanding of the human relation factors in work situations

12. From the above passage, it is MOST reasonable to conclude that when role-playing is used, it is preferable to have the roles acted out by

    A. only one set of actors
    B. no more than two sets of actors
    C. several different sets of actors
    D. the trainer or trainers of the group

13. Based on the above passage, a trainer using the technique of role reversal in a problem of first-line supervision should assign a senior enforcement agent to play the part of a(n)

    A. enforcement agent
    B. senior enforcement agent
    C. principal enforcement agent
    D. angry citizen

14. It can be inferred from the above passage that a *limitation* of role-play as a training method is that

    A. many work situations do not lend themselves to role-play
    B. employees are not experienced enough as actors to play the roles realistically
    C. only trainers who have psychological training can use it successfully
    D. participants who are observing and not acting do not benefit from it

15. To obtain good results from the use of role-play in training, a trainer should give participants

    A. a minimum of information about the situation so that they can act spontaneously
    B. scripts which illustrate the best method for handling the situation
    C. a complete explanation of the problem and the roles to be acted out
    D. a summary of work problems which involve interpersonal relations

Questions 16-20.

DIRECTIONS: Questions 16 through 20 are to be answered SOLELY on the basis of the following passage.

The dynamics of group behavior may be summed up by saying that the individuals in a group respond to many lines of force arising out of their relationship with every other member of a group and with the group itself. In addition, each member of a group quite naturally brings with him all the things that have been *bugging* him. Then, the situation or the setting in which the group meets, as well as the circumstances related to the formation of the group, are active working forces exerting some X influence upon each member of the group. Lastly, all of this kinetic energy is at the control of the person seeking to lead the group into some kind of action. If he is to produce something meaningful with the members of a group, he must utilize this energy, contain it, dissipate it in some fashion, or be faced with difficulty.

This dynamic force inherent in any group can be harnessed by a supervisor with leadership qualities, but it must be controlled. It will not be contained by acting without consultation with group members, by refusing to accept suggestions coming from the group, or by refusing to explain or even give notice of contemplated actions. However, it can be controlled by placing the focus upon the members of the group, rather than upon the supervisor, and depending upon the leader-supervisor to provide as many participative experiences for group members as is commensurate with his own decision-making responsibilities. It is true that this is subordinate-centered leadership, but the supervisor can gain strength through permissive leadership without sacrificing basic responsibilities for effective planning and adequate control of operations.

16. Of the following titles, the one that MOST closely describes the reading selection is

    A. THE SUPERVISOR WITH DYNAMIC LEADERSHIP POTENTIAL
    B. DISSIPATION OF GROUP ENERGY
    C. CONTROLLING GROUP RELATIONSHIPS
    D. SACRIFICING BASIC RESPONSIBILITIES

17. According to the above passage, the setting in which the group meets

    A. can readily be modified either in whole or in part
    B. must be made meaningful in some fashion to foster skills development
    C. can provide the sole source of group dynamics
    D. is one of the forces exerting influence on group members

18. According to the above passage, the members of the group

    A. should control their formation and development
    B. should control the circumstances of their meeting
    C. are influenced by the forces creating the group
    D. dissipate meaningless energy

19. According to the above passage, the effective group leader

    A. controls the focus of the group
    B. focuses his control over the group
    C. controls group forces by focusing upon group members
    D. focuses the group's forces upon himself

20. According to the above passage, effective leadership consists in

    A. partially compromising decision-making responsibilities
    B. partially sacrificing some basic responsibilities
    C. sometimes cultivating permissive subordinates
    D. providing participation for members of the group consistent with decision-making imperatives

Questions 21-22.

DIRECTIONS: Questions 21 and 22 are to be answered SOLELY on the basis of the following passage.

This country was built on the puritanical belief that honest toil was the foundation of moral rectitude, the cement of society, and the uphill road to progress. Idleness was sin. As a result, we treat free time today as a conditional joy. We permit outselves to relax only as a reward for hard work or as the recreation needed to put us back into shape for the job. Thus, the aimless delightful play of children gives way in adult life to a serious dedication to golf, the game that is so good for business.

21. According to the above passage, during former times in this country respectable work was considered to be MOST NEARLY a

    A. way to improve health
    B. form of recreation
    C. developer of good character
    D. reward for leisure

22. According to the point of view presented in the above passage, it would be MOST reasonable to assume that an employer would consider an employee's vacation to be a time for the employee to

    A. determine his own leisure time priorities
    B. loaf and relax
    C. learn new recreational skills
    D. increase his effectiveness at work

Questions 23-24.

DIRECTIONS: Questions 23 and 24 are to be answered SOLELY on the basis of the following passage.

A recent study revealed some very concrete evidence concerning the relationship between avocations and mental health. A number of well-adjusted persons were surveyed as to the type, number, and duration of their hobbies. The findings were compared to those from a similar survey of mentally disturbed persons. In the well-adjusted group, both the number of hobbies and the intensity with which they were pursued were far greater than that of the mentally disturbed group.

23. According to the above passage, the study showed that 23.____

    A. well-adjusted people engage in hobbies more widely and deeply than do mentally disturbed people
    B. hobbies, if taken seriously, serve to keep most people mentally well
    C. mental patients should be taught hobbies as a part of their therapy
    D. the degree of interest in hobbies plays an important role in maintaining good mental health

24. In reference to the study mentioned in the above passage, it is MOST accurate to say that it appears to have 24.____

    A. been based on a carefully-structured, complex research design
    B. considered the variables of mental health and hobby involvement
    C. contained a general definition of mental health
    D. given evidence of a causal relationship between hobbies and mental health

25. Across the years, our social sense has decreed that every position of social leadership, every place of influence, every concentration of social power in the hands of an individual, every instrument or agency that has aggregated to itself the power to affect the common welfare, has become by that very fact a social trust that must be administered for the common good. In our moral world, the social obligations of power are real and unescapable. On the basis of this statement, it would be MOST correct to state that 25.____

    A. an individual engaged in private enterprise does not have the social responsibility of one who holds public office
    B. social leadership carries with it the obligation to administer for the public good
    C. in our moral world, the abuse of the power is real and unescapable
    D. social leadership depends upon the aggregation of power in the hands of an individual or in an agency that wields concentrated influence

KEY (CORRECT ANSWERS)

1. B
2. C
3. A
4. C
5. C

6. A
7. A
8. A
9. C
10. C

11. D
12. C
13. A
14. A
15. C

16. C
17. D
18. C
19. C
20. D

21. C
22. D
23. A
24. B
25. B

TEST 2

DIRECTIONS: Each question or incomplete statement is followed by several suggested answers or completions. Select the one that BEST answers the question or completes the statement. *PRINT THE LETTER OF THE CORRECT ANSWER IN THE SPACE AT THE RIGHT.*

Questions 1-9.

DIRECTIONS: Questions 1 through 9 are to be answered SOLELY on the basis of the following passage.

    The establishment of a procedure whereby the client's rent is paid directly by the Social Service agency has been suggested recently by many people in the Social Service field. It is believed that such a procedure would be advantageous to both the agency and the client. Under the current system, clients often complain that their rent allowances are not for the correct amount. Agencies, in turn, have had to cope with irate landlords who complain that they are not receiving rent checks until much later than their due date.

    The proposed new system would involve direct payment of the client's rent by the agency to the landlord. Clients would not receive a monthly rent allowance. Under one possible implementation of such a system, special rent payment offices would be set up in each borough and staffed by Social Service clerical personnel. Each office would handle all work involved in sending out monthly rent payments. Each client would receive monthly notification from the Social Service agency that his rent has been paid. A rent office would be established for every three Social Service centers in each borough. Only in cases where the rental exceeds $350 per month would payment be made and records kept by the Social Service center itself rather than a special rent office. However, clients would continue to make all direct contacts through the Social Service center.

    Files in the rent offices would be organized on the basis of client rental. All cases involving monthly rents up to, but not exceeding, $300 would be placed in salmon-colored folders. Cases with rents from $300 to $500 would be placed in buff folders, and those with rents exceeding $500, but less than $750 would be filed in blue folders. If a client's rental changed, he would be required to notify the center as soon as possible so that this information could be brought up-to-date in his folder and the color of his folder changed if necessary. Included in the information needed, in addition to the amount of rent, are the size of the apartment, the type of heat, and the number of flights of stairs to climb if there is no elevator.

    Discussion as to whether the same information should be required of clients residing in city projects was resolved with the decision that the identical system of filing and updating of files should apply to such project tenants. The basic problem that might arise from the institution of such a program is that clients would resent being unable to pay their own rent. However, it is likely that such resentment would be only a temporary reaction to change and would disappear after the new system became standard procedure. It has been suggested that this program first be experimented with on a small scale to determine what problems may arise and how the program can be best implemented.

1. According to the above passage, there a number of complaints about the current system of rent payments. Which of the following is a complaint expressed in the passage?

1.____

A. Landlords complain that clients sometimes pay the wrong amount for their rent.
B. Landlords complain that clients sometimes do not pay their rent on time.
C. Clients say that the Social Service agency sometimes does not mail the rent out on time.
D. Landlords say that they sometimes fail to receive a check for the rent.

2. Assume that there are 15 Social Service centers in Manhattan.
According to the above passage, the number of rent offices that should be established in that borough under the new system is

   A. 1   B. 3   C. 5   D. 15

3. According to the above passage, a client under the new system would receive

   A. a rent receipt from the landlord indicating that Social Services has paid the rent
   B. nothing since his rent has been paid by Social Services
   C. verification from the landlord that the rent was paid
   D. notices of rent payment from the Social Service agency

4. According to the above passage, a case record involving a client whose rent has changed from $310 to $540 per month should be changed from a _____ folder to a _____ folder.

   A. blue; salmon-colored   B. buff; blue
   C. salmon-colored; blue   D. yellow; buff

5. According to the above passage, if a client's rental is lowered because of violations in his building, he would be required to notify the

   A. building department   B. landlord
   C. rent payment office   D. Social Service center

6. Which one of the following kinds of information about a rented apartment is NOT mentioned in the above passage as being necessary to include in the client's folder?
The

   A. floor number, if in an apartment house with an elevator
   B. rental, if in a city project apartment
   C. size of the apartment, if in a two-family house
   D. type of heat, if in a city project apartment

7. Assume that the rent payment proposal discussed in the above passage is approved and ready for implementation in the city.
Which of the following actions is MOST in accordance with the proposal described in the above passage?

   A. Change over completely and quickly to the new system to avoid the confusion of having clients under both systems.
   B. Establish rent payment offices in all of the existing Social Service centers.
   C. Establish one small rent payment office in Manhattan for about six months.
   D. Set up an office in each borough and discontinue issuing rent allowances.

8. According to the above passage, it can be inferred that the MOST important drawback of the new system would be that once a program is started clients might feel

A. they have less independence than they had before
B. unable to cope with problems that mature people should be able to handle
C. too far removed from Social Service personnel to successfully adapt to the new requirements
D. too independent to work with the system

9. The above passage suggests that the proposed rent program be started as a pilot program rather than be instituted immediately throughout the city.
Of the following possible reasons for a pilot program, the one which is stated in the above passage as the MOST direct reason is that

A. any change made would then be only on a temporary basis
B. difficulties should be determined from small-scale implementation
C. implementation on a wide scale is extremely difficult
D. many clients might resent the new system

Questions 10-14.

DIRECTIONS: Questions 10 through 14 are to be answered SOLELY on the basis of the following passage.

PROCEDURE TO OBTAIN REIMBURSEMENT FROM DEPARTMENT OF HEALTH
FOR CARE OF PHYSICALLY HANDICAPPED CHILDREN

Application for reimbursement must be received by the Department of Health within 30 days of the date of hospital admission in order that the Department of Hospitals may be reimbursed from the date of admission. Upon determination that patient is physically handicapped, as defined under Chapter 780 of the State Laws, the ward clerk shall prepare seven copies of Department of Health Form A-1 or A-2, Application and Authorization, and shall submit six copies to the institutional Collections Unit. The ward clerk shall also initiate two copies of Department of Health Form B-1 or B-2, Financial and Social Report, and shall forward them to the institutional Collections Unit for completion of Page 1 and routing to the Social Service Division for completion of the Social Summary on Page 2. Social Service Division shall return Form B-1 or B-2 to the institutional Collections Unit which shall forward one copy of Form B-1 or B-2 and six copies of Form A-1 or A-2 to Central Office Division of Collections for transmission to Bureau of Handicapped Children, Department of Health.

10. According to the above paragraph, the Department of Health will pay for hospital care for

A. children who are physically handicapped
B. any children who are ward patients
C. physically handicapped adults and children
D. thirty days for eligible children

11. According to the procedure described in the above paragraph, the definition of what constitutes a physical handicap is made by the

A. attending physician
B. laws of the State
C. Social Service Division
D. ward clerk

12. According to the above paragraph, Form B-1 or B-2 is   12.____
    A. a three page form containing detachable pages
    B. an authorization form issued by the Department of Hospitals
    C. completed by the ward clerk after the Social Summary has been entered
    D. sent to the institutional Collections Unit by the Social Service Division

13. According to the above paragraph, after their return by the Social Service Division, the   13.____
    institutional Collections Unit keeps
    A. one copy of Form A-1 or A-2
    B. one copy of Form A-1 or A-2 and one copy of Form B-1 or B-2
    C. one copy of Form B-1 or B-2
    D. no copies of Forms A-1 or A-2 or B-1 or B-2

14. According to the above paragraph, forwarding the *Application and Authorization* to the   14.____
    Department of Health is the responsibility of the
    A. Bureau for Handicapped Children
    B. Central Office Division of Collections
    C. Institutional Collections Unit
    D. Social Service Division

Questions 15-19.

DIRECTIONS: Questions 15 through 19 are to be answered SOLELY on the basis of the following *total annual income adjustment* rules for household income.

The basic annual income is to be calculated by multiplying the total of the current weekly salaries of all adults (age 21 or over) by 52.

Upward and downward adjustments must be made to the basic annual salary to arrive at the *total adjusted annual income* for the household.

UPWARD ADJUSTMENTS

1. Add one-half of total overtime payments in the previous two years.
2. Add that part of the earnings of any minor in the household that exceeded $3,000 in the previous 12 months.

DOWNWARD ADJUSTMENTS

1. Deduct one-third of all educational tuition payments for household members in the previous 12 months.
2. Deduct the expense of going to and from work in excess of $30 per week per household member. This adjustment is made on the basis of the previous 12 months and should be computed for each household member individually for each week in which excess travel expenses were incurred.
3. Deduct that part of child care expenses which exceeded $1,500 in the previous 12 months.

15. In Household A, the husband has a weekly salary of $585 and the wife has just had her salary increased from $390 to $420 per week. In the previous 12 months, each had a paid continuous vacation of four weeks; the husband had to travel to a secondary work location every fourth week. His travel costs during those weeks were $42 per week. In the previous 12 months, they had child care costs of $1,470.
What is the TOTAL annual adjusted income for the household?

   A. $52,116   B. $52,104   C. $51,828   D. $51,234

16. In Household B, the husband has a weekly salary of $540. In the past year, he received overtime payments of $255. In the year before that, he received overtime payments of $1,221. His wife has just begun a job with a weekly salary of $330. As a result of this, annual child care expenses will be $2,130.
What is the TOTAL annual adjusted income for the household?

   A. $45,240   B. $45,348   C. $45,978   D. $46,824

17. In Household C, the husband has a weekly salary of $555. The wife has a weekly salary of $390. They each had expenses of $33 per week when traveling to and from work in the previous 12 months. The husband had an annual paid vacation of five weeks, and the wife had an annual paid vacation of three weeks in the previous year. There is a daughter in college for whom annual tuition payments of $1,710 were made in the previous 12 months.
What is the TOTAL annual adjusted income for the household?

   A. $48,258   B. $48,282   C. $49,140   D. $50,022

18. In Household D, the husband has a weekly salary of $465, the wife has a weekly salary of $330, and an adult daughter has a weekly salary of $285. The husband received overtime payments of $1,890 in the past year. In the year before that, he received no overtime payments. In the past year, there were weekly child care expenses of $210 per week for 47 weeks.
What is the TOTAL adjusted annual income for the household?

   A. $57,105   B. $48,735   C. $47,235   D. $46,845

19. In Household E, the husband has a weekly salary of $615. The wife has a weekly salary of $195. During the past year, there were tuition payments of $255 per month for 10 months per year for children in grade school and annual tuition payments of $2,310 for a boy in high school. What is the TOTAL adjusted annual income for the household?

   A. $39,570   B. $39,690   C. $40,500   D. $42,120

Questions 20-22.

DIRECTIONS: Questions 20 through 22 are to be answered SOLELY on the basis of the following paragraph.

Effective December 1, 2004, tenants thereafter admitted to public housing projects shall pay rents in accordance with Schedule DV if they are veterans of the Gulf War, and in accordance with Schedule D if they are not Gulf War veterans. However, all recipients of public assistance shall pay rents in accordance with Schedule DW. Tenants of public housing projects prior to the effective date of this change will continue to pay rent in accordance with Schedule C2 if they are veterans of the Iraqi War or the Gulf War, in accordance with

Schedule C if they are not such veterans, and in accordance with Schedule CW if they receive public assistance and if they are not eligible to use the C2 Schedule. In addition, effective December 1, 2004, when a tenant is accepted for assistance by the Department of Welfare, if such acceptance requires that the tenant pay a new rental as outlined above, the effective date of the new rental is to be the first of the month following the date that the tenant is accepted for assistance by the Department of Welfare instead of the first of the month following the date of application for public assistance.

20. John Jones, a Gulf War veteran, has been living in a public housing project since June 2003. He applied for public assistance on November 15, 2004 and was accepted for public assistance on December 17, 2004.
If he continues to receive public assistance, his present rent should be based on the _____ Schedule.

   A. C2 B. CW C. DV D. DW

21. Jack Smith, who is not a veteran, moves into a public housing project in January 2006. If it should become necessary for him to apply for public assistance on February 10, 2006 and should he be accepted for such assistance on March 5, 2006, the rent that he pays in March 2006 should be based on the _____ Schedule.

   A. C B. CW C. D D. DW

22. John Doe, a veteran of the Iraqi War, was admitted to a public housing project in August 2004. He applied for public assistance on February 1, 2005 and was accepted for such assistance on March 1, 2005.
On April 1, 2005, his rent should

   A. change to the C2 Schedule
   B. remain on the C2 Schedule, as previously
   C. change to the CW Schedule
   D. remain on the CW Schedule, as previously

Questions 23-25.

DIRECTIONS: Questions 23 through 25 are to be answered SOLELY on the basis of the following paragraph.

It has been proposed that an act be passed to provide for family allowances in the form of cash payments, normally to mothers, for children under sixteen years of age. Allowances are supposed to be spent exclusively for the care and education of the children; otherwise, they may be discontinued. They would vary in amount according to the age of the child and would be conditional upon satisfactory school attendance and accomplishment. The allowance would be paid to all families, regardless of means, but income tax exemptions for dependents would be reduced in consequence. The act would also permit the withdrawal of children from school and their entrance into the labor market after completing eighth grade. However, there would be no financial advantage in sending a child to work since the allowances would approximate the child's net earnings. Proponents of this proposal claim as advantages that it would provide social justice by taking into account elements of family need not possible under any normal wage structure system, be simple to administer, encourage an increase in the birth rate, remove unwilling or incapable students from our middle schools, and provide financial aid to poor, large families without the stigma of public welfare.

23. According to the proposal, the one of the following factors which would be LEAST likely to cause a variation in the amount of the allowance to a family or cause a discontinuance of it is

    A. a change in family wealth
    B. poor school attendance record of a child
    C. a child's being left back
    D. use of the allowance money on a hobby of one of the parents

    23._____

24. The LEAST accurate of the following statements concerning schooling under this proposal is:

    A. A 14-year-old girl attending the 6th grade of elementary school will not be permitted to leave school, even though her school work is unsatisfactory.
    B. A poor family will be encouraged to continue the schooling of their 15-year-old twins who are in the junior year of high school.
    C. A 14-year-old boy who has been graduated from elementary school, but whose school attendance has been unsatisfactory, will not be permitted to attend high school.
    D. The family of a 17-year-old high school senior who is an honor student will not receive an allowance.

    24._____

25. College attendance of bright children of poor families may be aided by this proposal because

    A. such children will be assured of higher marks
    B. families are likely to be smaller and consequently parents will be better able to send their children to college
    C. more scholarships are likely to be offered by private colleges as a result of this proposal
    D. the financial subsidy granted for a child under 16 may help the family save money towards a college education

    25._____

KEY (CORRECT ANSWERS)

1.	B	11.	B
2.	C	12.	D
3.	D	13.	C
4.	B	14.	B
5.	D	15.	A
6.	A	16.	C
7.	C	17.	B
8.	A	18.	B
9.	B	19.	C
10.	A	20.	A

21. C
22. B
23. A
24. C
25. D

FORMS

EXAMINATION SECTION
TEST 1

DIRECTIONS: Each question or incomplete statement is followed by several suggested answers or completions. Select the one that BEST answers the question or completes the statement. *PRINT THE LETTER OF THE CORRECT ANSWER IN THE SPACE AT THE RIGHT.*

Questions 1-10.

DIRECTIONS: Questions 1 through 10 are to be answered on the basis of the information and the form given below.

The form below is a Daily Summary of Clinic Visits and lists ten persons who used a clinic in Washington Hospital on September 4. The form includes the following information about each patient: name, identification number, date of birth, case number, fee, and bill number.

SEPTEMBER 4
WASHINGTON HOSPITAL - DAILY SUMMARY OF CLINIC VISITS

Name of Patient Last, First	Identification Number	Date of Birth Mo.	Day	Yr.	Case Number	Fee	Bill Number
Enders, John	89-4143-67	08	01	41	434317	$ 90.00	129631
Dawes, Mary	71-6142-69	11	17	36	187963	$ 47.50	129632
Lang, Donald	54-1213-73	10	07	45	897436	$ 180.00	129633
Eiger, Alan	18-7649-63	06	19	21	134003	$ 110.00	129634
Ramirez, Jose	61-4319-69	03	30	66	379030	$ 130.00	129635
Ilono, Frank	13-9161-57	08	19	53	565645	$ 66.00	129636
Sloan, Irene	55-8643-66	05	13	27	799732	$ 112.50	129637
Long, Thomas	41-3963-74	12	03	46	009784	$ 37.50	129638
McKay, Cathy	14-9633-44	05	09	36	000162	$ 96.00	129639
Dale, Sarah	86-1113-69	11	13	29	543211	$ 138.00	129640

1. The fee for Cathy McKay is LESS than the fee for   1.____

   A. John Enders   B. Alan Eiger
   C. Frank Ilono   D. Thomas Long

2. The two patients who were born in the same year are   2.____

   A. John Enders and Frank Ilono
   B. Mary Dawes and Sarah Dale
   C. Donald Lang and Thomas Long
   D. Cathy McKay and Mary Dawes

3. The case number for Irene Sloan is   3.____

   A. 979732   B. 799372   C. 799732   D. 797732

4. Cathy McKay's identification number is

   A. 44-9633-14   B. 14-9633-44
   C. 000162   D. 129639

5. Frank Ilono's case number is

   A. 556645   B. 565465   C. 565645   D. 565654

6. The bill numbers for Jose Ramirez and Thomas Long are

   A. 129635 and 129638   B. 129635 and 129683
   C. 129634 and 129638   D. 129634 and 129637

7. The fees for Donald Lang, Sarah Dale, and Mary Dawes are

   A. $47.50, $180.00, $96.00
   B. $110.00, $138.00, $90.00
   C. $180, $130, $47.50
   D. $180, $138, $47.50

8. The case numbers for Thomas Long and Mary Dawes are

   A. 009784 and 187963   B. 090784 and 187963
   C. 009784 and 187693   D. 009874 and 187963

9. The identification numbers for Fra.nk Ilono and Donald Lang are

   A. 13-9161-57 and 54-1312-73
   B. 54-1213-73 and 13-6191-57
   C. 13-9161-57 and 54-1213-73
   D. 54-1213-37 and 13-9161-57

10. The birth dates of Irene Sloan, John Enders, and Sarah Dale are

    A. 05/31/27, 01/08/41, and 11/13/39
    B. 05/13/37, 08/01/41, and 11/13/39
    C. 05/31/27, 01/08/41, and 11/13/29
    D. 05/13/27, 08/01/41, and 11/13/29

Questions 11-17.

DIRECTIONS: Questions 11 through 17 are to be answered SOLELY on the basis of the information below and the form shown on the following page.

The following form is a Weekly Summary of New Employees and lists all employees appointed to Department F in the week indicated. In addition to the starting date and name, the form includes each new employee's time card number, title, status, work location, and supervisor's name.

	DEPARTMENT F				
Weekly Summary of New Employees				Week Starting March 25	
Starting Date	Name Last, First	Time Card No.	Title	Status	Work Location	Supervisor
3/25	Astaire, Hannah	361	Typist	Prov.	Rm. 312	Merrill, Judy
3/25	Silber, Arthur	545	Clerk	Perm.	Rm. 532	Rizzo, Joe
3/26	Vecchio, Robert	620	Accountant	Perm.	Rm. 620	Harper, Ruth
3/26	Goldberg, Sally	373	Stenographer	Prov.	Rm. 308	Merrill, Judy
3/26	Yee, Bruce	555	Accountant	Perm.	Rm. 530	Rizzo, Joe
3/27	Dunning, Betty	469	Typist	Perm.	Rm. 411	Miller, Tony
3/28	Goldman, Sara	576	Stenographer	Prov.	Rm. 532	Rizzo, Joe
3/29	Vesquez, Roy	624	Accountant	Perm.	Rm. 622	Harper, Ruth
3/29	Browning, David	464	Typist	Perm.	Rm. 411	Miller, Tony

11. On which one of the following dates did two employees *in the same title* begin work? 11.____

    A. 3/25   B. 3/26   C. 3/27   D. 3/29

12. To which one of the following supervisors was ONE typist assigned? 12.____

    A. Judy Merrill   B. Tony Miller
    C. Ruth Harper   D. Joe Rizzo

13. Which one of the following supervisors was assigned the GREATEST number of new employees during the week of March 25? 13.____

    A. Ruth Harper   B. Judy Merrill
    C. Tony Miller   D. Joe Rizzo

14. Which one of the following employees was assigned *three days after another employee* to the same job location? 14.____

    A. Sara Goldman   B. David Browning
    C. Bruce Yee   D. Roy Vesquez

15. The title in which BOTH provisional and permanent appointments were made is 15.____

    A. Accountant   B. Clerk
    C. Stenographer   D. Typist

16. The employees who started work on the same day and have the same status but different titles are 16.____

    A. Arthur Silber and Hannah Astaire
    B. Robert Vecchio and Bruce Yee
    C. Sally Goldberg and Sara Goldman
    D. Roy Vesquez and David Browning

17. On the basis of the information given on the form, which one of the following conclusions regarding time card numbers appears to be CORRECT?

    A. The first digit of the time card number is coded according to the assigned title.
    B. The middle digit of the time card number is coded according to the assigned title.
    C. The first digit of the time card number is coded according to the employees' floor locations.
    D. Time card numbers are randomly assigned.

17.____

Questions 18-19.

DIRECTIONS: Questions 18 and 19 are to be answered on the basis of the form which appears on the following page.

| INJURY TO INMATE REPORT | DEPARTMENT OF CORRECTION | INSTITUTION: Correctional | DATE: 6/15 |

INSTRUCTIONS: Original And One Copy — Original To Legal Division — Copy To Inmate Folder.

TO BE COMPLETED BY EMPLOYEE: Please Print.

1. **INMATE** → Name: John Doe | Number: 441-77-9375 | Location: 7M | Work: None

2. **DETAILS:** Inmate involved in altercation with inmate Henry Green #441-77-1656 in the rear of the 7M dormitory at approximately 6:15 p.m.

3. **EMPLOYEE** → I (DID) (DID NOT) WITNESS THIS INJURY. Signature: Arthur Kinney | Shield/ID No. 6214 | Title: C.O.

TO BE COMPLETED BY MEDICAL STAFF

4. **NATURE OF INJURY AND CAUSE:** Date Of Injury: 6-15 | Reported For Medical Attention DATE: 6-15 TIME: 7:30 a.m.

5. Presents discoloration to (L) jaw with small laceration to (L) lower lip. Puncture wound to (L) upper arm.

TREATMENT: Two sutures to (L) lower lip and order for x-ray to (L) jaw. Tetanus toxoid - dressing to puncture wound.

DISPOSITION: ☐ RETURN TO HOUSING AREA ☐ WORK RELEASE ___ DAYS ☐ LIGHT DUTY ___ DAYS ☐ RETURN TO DUTY ☐ RE-EXAM. ___ DAYS ☐ REFER TO CLINIC
☒ TRANSFER TO HOSPITAL — Name Of Hospital: Harmony
☐ OTHER (SPECIFY)

6. **TREATED BY** → Signature: James White, Title: M.D. | CHIEF MEDICAL OFFICER → Signature:

INMATE CERTIFICATION
I CERTIFY THAT THE CAUSE OF INJURY AS STATED HEREIN IS TO MY KNOWLEDGE TRUE AND MEDICAL ATTENTION WAS PROVIDED.

7. **INMATE** → Signature: John Doe | Number: 441-77-9375 | Date: 6.15
WITNESSED BY → Signature: John Day | Shield/ID No. 8756 | Title: C.O. | Date: 6.15

TO BE COMPLETED BY INVESTIGATING OFFICER

8. **INVESTIGATORS REPORT:** Inmate was involved in an altercation with inmate Henry Green #441-77-1656 in the rear area at the 7M Dorm. Attempt to elicit witnesses among inmate population proved futile. Inmate treated as above.
INVESTIGATING OFFICER → Signature: Ronald Doaks | Title: Captain | Shield No. 529 | Date: 6/15

HEAD OF INSTITUTION OR DIVISION
REMARKS:
HEAD OF INSTITUTION OR DIVISION → Signature: | Title: | Date:

18. Which one of the following numbered sections from the above Injury to Inmate Report contains information NOT consistent with information in the Tour Commander's report? 18.___

    A. 1   B. 3   C. 5   D. 7

19. Following are numbers of three sections from the above Injury to Inmate Report, which contains information which may or may not be justifiable according to the Tour Commander's report:

        Section 2
        Section 7
        Section 8

Which one of the following statements BEST describes the above sections?

    A. 7 and 8 are justifiable, but 2 is not.
    B. 2 and 8 are justifiable, but 7 is not.
    C. 2 and 7 are justifiable, but 8 is not.
    D. 2, 7, and 8 are all justifiable.

Questions 20-25.

DIRECTIONS: Questions 20 through 25 are to be answered on the basis of the form below.

METROPOLITAN CITY		
Last Name	First Name	Middle Initial Smith
	John	G.
Street		Apartment
758 Reason Street		1C
Borough or Town	State	Zip Code
Bronx	New York	10403
Monthly Rent	Number of Rooms	
$110.00	5	
FAMILY COMPOSITION				
Name	Relation to Head	Birth Date Mo./Yr.	Annual Income	Employer or School
1. Smith, John G.	Head	7/48	$52000	Harris Chemical
2. Smith, Ethel S.	Wife	3/51	0	
3. Smith, Lucy M.	Daughter	4/71	0	P.S. 172
4. Smith, John G., Jr.	Son	8/73	0	P.S. 172
5. Smith, Susan F.	Daughter	1/78	0	
6. Simmons, Sylvia T.	Mother in-law	4/30	$23400	F. W. Woolworth
7.				
Total Annual Income $75400				
Total Assets: Small Savings Accounts. $50,000 life insurance on Mr. Smith				
Additional Information _____				

20. The occupants of the Smith apartment are Mr. Smith, Mrs. Smith,

    A. her mother, their son and daughters
    B. his mother, their son and daughters
    C. her mother, their sons and daughter
    D. her mother, their sons and daughters

21. The income of the Smith household comes from the earnings of the father, the   21.____

    A. mother, the mother-in-law, and the children
    B. mother, and the children, but not the mother-in-law
    C. mother-in-law, and the children, but not the mother
    D. mother-in-law, but not the mother and children

22. From the information given about the Smith family, their apartment seems to be   22.____

    A. too small   B. the right size
    C. a little large   D. much too large

23. If an assistant goes to the Smiths' apartment to discuss their relocation and everyone is   23.____
    home except Mr. Smith, with whom should the assistant talk about relocation?

    A. John Jr. and Ethel Smith
    B. Ethel Smith and Sylvia Simmons
    C. Lucy and Ethel Smith
    D. John Smith, Jr. and Sylvia Simmons

24. The reason why the last column was left blank for Susan Smith is PROBABLY that   24.____

    A. the assistant forgot to ask for this information
    B. Susan's parents would not give this information
    C. Susan is too young to go to school
    D. Susan does not live at home

25. The section for Additional Information was left blank MOST probably because   25.____

    A. the assistant did not have time to ask for more information
    B. the Smith family is sufficiently well-described by the other information on the form
    C. the Additional Information section is not an important part of the form
    D. unfavorable facts have been purposely left out

KEY (CORRECT ANSWERS)

1.	B	11.	B
2.	D	12.	A
3.	C	13.	D
4.	B	14.	A
5.	C	15.	D
6.	A	16.	D
7.	D	17.	C
8.	A	18.	B
9.	C	19.	A
10.	D	20.	A

21. D
22. A
23. B
24. C
25. B

TEST 2

DIRECTIONS: Each question or incomplete statement is followed by several suggested answers or completions. Select the one that BEST answers the question or completes the statement. *PRINT THE LETTER OF THE CORRECT ANSWER IN THE SPACE AT THE RIGHT.*

Questions 1-7.

DIRECTIONS: Questions 1 through 7 are to be answered SOLELY on the basis of the information and the sample report given below.

    S. Perez and W. Carr, counselors in Dormitory C-4 at Robinson Juvenile Center, are on duty in the dormitory on September 17, 2009. At 10:15 A.M., a child suddenly begins screaming in Room 211. W. Carr runs to the room and finds a child, Bobbie Doe, lying on the floor. The child who is screaming is Bobbie Doe's roommate, Leslie Roe. Leslie says that they were both jumping on the beds, and Bobbie landed wrong and fell on the floor. Bobbie is moaning now and saying, *I sure landed hard. My head hurts.* The counselor sees that there is a slight amount of blood on the back of Bobbie's head and sends Bobbie to Dr. J. Field in the medical unit to be checked for head injury and other possible injuries. As soon as Bobbie has arrived safely at the medical unit, the counselor fills out the following form.

```
┌─────────────────────────────────────────────────────────────────┐
│                    REPORT OF ACCIDENT TO CHILD                  │
│                     (to be filled out in triplicate)            │
│  1. Name of injured child _____ │
│  2. Date of injury _____ 3. Time _____ │
│  4. Describe how injury occurred _____ │
│  5. Signature of counselor _____ 6. Date _____ │
│ TO  BE FILLED IN BY MEDICAL UNIT: _____ │
│  7. Nature of injury _____ │
│  8. Treatment given _____ │
│  9. Further treatment needed _____ │
│ 10. Signature of physician or nurse _____ 11. Date _____ │
└─────────────────────────────────────────────────────────────────┘
```

1. How many copies of the *Report of Accident to Child* is the counselor supposed to make out?

   A. 1   B. 2   C. 3   D. 4

2. Which of the following names is the CORRECT entry for Item 1 of the report form?

   A. S. Perez   B. W. Carr
   C. Leslie Roe   D. Bobbie Doe

3. Which of the following is the CORRECT entry for Item 2 of the report form?

   A. 9/17/09   B. 10/17/09   C. 10:15 A.M.   D. 10:15 P.M.

4. An accurate report of the cause of an injury is important for two purposes: First, it gives the medical unit an idea of what kinds of injuries should be looked for; second, it is a record of who or what was responsible for the accident.
   Which one of the following entries for Item 4 BEST fulfills both of these purposes?

123

A. Child complained, *My head hurts.* Investigation showed some bleeding.
B. Child was jumping on bed and fell on floor. Child reported that his head was hurt. Head was bleeding slightly.
C. Child's roommate reported they had been jumping on beds. This behavior is dangerous, and it is against the rules.
D. Child's roommate began screaming when child was hurt. Counselor found child lying on floor and moaning.

5. Which of the following names is the CORRECT entry for Item 5 of the report form? 5._____

   A. S. Perez   B. W. Carr
   C. Leslie Roe   D. J. Field

6. Which of the following is the CORRECT entry for Item 6? 6._____

   A. September, A.M., 2009   B. September 2009, 10:15 A.M.
   C. September 17, 2009   D. September 2009, Robinson

7. What information, if any, should the counselor fill in for Item 7? 7._____

   A. Head injury
   B. Injuries from falling on floor
   C. Head injury and possible other injuries
   D. No information

Questions 8-12.

DIRECTIONS: Questions 8 through 12 are to be answered SOLELY on the basis of the information below and the sample form given on the following page.

When children are admitted to a juvenile detention center, all their personal property, including the clothing that they are wearing, is taken away from them. A record is kept of this property on the following Personal Property List; and when they leave the center, all their personal property is returned to them.

SAMPLE FORM FOR LISTING PERSONAL PROPERTY

PERSONAL PROPERTY LIST			
Item	Color	Material	Quantity
Shirt			
Pants			
Belt			
Undershorts			
Undershirt			
Socks			
Sneakers			
Shoes			
Sandals			
Coat			
Hat			
Sweater			
Other (describe)			
Name of Child _____ Admission Date _____			

Two children, Allen Adams and Bertram Brown, were admitted to Juvenile Center X on October 1, 2009. An admissions counselor found that they had the following items of personal property:

ALLEN ADAMS - 1 pair white cotton socks, 1 pair blue sneakers, blue cotton shirt, tan wool pants, brown vinyl belt, white cotton undershorts, white cotton undershirt, wristwatch, brown wool sweater, and a ballpoint pen.

BERTRAM BROWN - 1 pair black cotton socks, 1 pair white sneakers, white polyester shirt, tan cotton pants, white cotton undershorts, white cotton undershirt, tan leather coat, brown plastic wallet with bus pass and 50¢ in change.

8. Which of the following is the MOST complete and correct entry for *Shirt* on the Personal Property List for Allen Adams?

    A. White, cotton, one
    B. Blue, wool, one
    C. Blue, cotton, one
    D. White, polyester, one

9. If, at the time of admission, the child does not have with him or is not wearing one of the items listed, the line for that item is left blank.
Which one of the following items should be left BLANK on the Personal Property List for Bertram Brown?

    A. Pants   B. Belt   C. Sneakers   D. Other

10. Which of the following is the MOST complete and correct entry for *other* on the Personal Property List for Allen Adams?

    A. Wristwatch, one; Ballpoint pen, one
    B. Wristwatch, one; Ballpoint pen, one; Sweater, brown, wool, one
    C. Socks, white, cotton, one; Sweater, brown, wool, one
    D. Socks, white, cotton, one; Wristwatch, one; Brown sweater, wool, one

11. For which of the following items should there be NO entry on the Personal Property List either for Allen Adams or for Bertram Brown?

    A. Undershorts
    B. Sneakers
    C. Coat
    D. Hat

12. Allen Adams and Bertram Brown have two items of personal property that are identical in kind, color, and quantity. These two items are

    A. Shirt; Pants
    B. Undershorts; Socks
    C. Pants; Undershorts
    D. Undershirt; Undershorts

Questions 13-17.

DIRECTIONS: Questions 13 through 17 are to be answered SOLELY on the basis of the information and the sample report form given below.

On the evening of Wednesday, October 30, 2009, a counselor is making a routine check of Dormitory A-3 at Smith Juvenile Center. In checking the bathroom, the counselor discovers that a sink is full of water and is starting to overflow onto the floor. The cold water tap is leaking, and the sink is not draining. The counselor finds a wad of paper blocking the sink drain. When the paper is removed, the sink drains immediately. However, the cold water tap cannot be turned off. The counselor goes to the desk and begins to fill out the following Repair

Request Form. The counselor making the repair request is L. Rolin. The other counselor on duty in Dormitory A-3 is A. Pollitt. The department head for this dormitory is S. Jones.

```
REPAIR REQUEST FORM
A.  Name of Juvenile Center _____
B.  Exact location of repair job _____
C.  Date _____
D.  Type of condition requiring repair _____
E.  Signature of staff member requesting repair _____
F.  Signature of department head approving _____
G.  Signature of repair worker and date repair completed _____
                                                    _____(Date)_____
```

13. The information that should be indicated on Line B of the Repair Request Form is

    A. Smith Juvenile Center
    B. Dormitory A
    C. Sink, Smith Juvenile Center
    D. Bathroom, Dormitory A-3

14. Which of the following is the MOST exact and informative entry for Line C?

    A. Wednesday evening   B. 2009
    C. October 2009   D. October 30, 2009

15. Which of the following entries for Line D should be the MOST useful to a repair supervisor in deciding what kind of repair worker should make the repair and what equipment the worker should have?

    A. Sink was discovered overflowing onto floor
    B. Cold water tap is leaking
    C. Cold water tap is dripping and sink is not draining
    D. Sink drain is plugged up

16. The person whose signature should appear on Line E is

    A. L. Rolin   B. A. Pollitt
    C. S. Jones   D. the repair worker

17. A line on the Repair Request Form that CANNOT be filled out on the basis of the information given above is Line

    A. A   B. D   C. F   D. G

Questions 18-25.

DIRECTIONS: Questions 18 through 25 are to be answered SOLELY on the basis of the information and the form given below.

On February 2, at 2:45 P.M., a white male, 45 years old, was received at the mortuary and placed in Compartment 121. He was brought in by Ambulance No. 3, driven by James Earl. The ambulance had been summoned by Patrolman Teddy Cordello, Shield No. 143, of the 41st Precinct. According to Cordello, the deceased, John Smith, had died in the street after being hit by a car. Among his effects was a letter postmarked February 1. Smith's body was claimed by his sister, Susan Crown, accompanied by Sidney Crawford, an undertaker, on February 3 at 1:15 P.M. At that time, Permit Number 376 was

MORTUARY MASTER INDEX CARD				
Index No.	1. Name	2. Comp. No.	3. Color	4. Age
Photo-Date	Cert. Issued	Anatomical	Identification	
			Waived	F. Prints
			Personal	Unverified
Hold Request		5. Place of Death	6. Received From Date of Death	
7. Date Rec'd		8. Date Claimed	9. Time Claimed Permit No.	
To: City Mortuary M.E. Case No.			10. Claimant	11. Undertaker
Forms		Received by _____	Checked with _____	
File Prepared by _____				
Completed by _____				
Remarks:				

18. For Item 2, the CORRECT entry is

    A. 121 B. 143 C. 376 D. 112

19. For Item 4, the CORRECT entry is

    A. 36 B. 45 C. 46 D. 54

20. For Item 5, the CORRECT entry is

    A. home B. office C. street D. hospital

21. For Item 7, the CORRECT entry is

    A. Feb. 1 B. Feb. 2 C. Feb. 3 D. Feb. 4

22. For Item 8, the CORRECT entry is

    A. Feb. 1 B. Feb. 2 C. Feb. 3 D. Feb. 4

23. For Item 9, the CORRECT entry is

    A. 1:15 A.M. B. 2:45 A.M. C. 1:15 P.M. D. 2:45 P.M.

24. For Item 10, the CORRECT entry is

    A. John Smith B. Susan Crown
    C. Sidney Crawford D. Susan Smith

25. For Item 11, the CORRECT entry is

    A. Susan Crawford B. John Smith
    C. Sidney Crawford D. Susan Crown

KEY (CORRECT ANSWERS)

1. C
2. D
3. A
4. B
5. B

6. C
7. D
8. C
9. B
10. A

11. D
12. D
13. D
14. D
15. A

16. A
17. D
18. A
19. B
20. C

21. B
22. C
23. C
24. B
25. C

PREPARING WRITTEN MATERIAL

PARAGRAPH REARRANGEMENT
COMMENTARY

The sentences that follow are in scrambled order. You are to rearrange them in proper order and indicate the letter choice containing the correct answer at the space at the right.

Each group of sentences in this section is actually a paragraph presented in scrambled order. Each sentence in the group has a place in that paragraph; no sentence is to be left out. You are to read each group of sentences and decide upon the best order in which to put the sentences so as to form a well-organized paragraph.

The questions in this section measure the ability to solve a problem when all the facts relevant to its solution are not given.

More specifically, certain positions of responsibility and authority require the employee to discover connection between events sometimes, apparently, unrelated. In order to do this, the employee will find it necessary to correctly infer that unspecified events have probably occurred or are likely to occur. This ability becomes especially important when action must be taken on incomplete information.

Accordingly, these questions require competitors to choose among several suggested alternatives, each of which presents a different sequential arrangement of the events. Competitors must choose the MOST logical of the suggested sequences.

In order to do so, they may be required to draw on general knowledge to infer missing concepts or events that are essential to sequencing the given events. Competitors should be careful to infer only what is essential to the sequence. The plausibility of the wrong alternatives will always require the inclusion of unlikely events or of additional chains of events which are NOT essential to sequencing the given events.

It's very important to remember that you are looking for the best of the four possible choices, and that the best choice of all may not even be one of the answers you're given to choose from.

There is no one right way to solve these problems. Many people have found it helpful to first write out the order of the sentences, as they would have arranged them, on their scrap paper before looking at the possible answers. If their optimum answer is there, this can save them some time. If it isn't, this method can still give insight into solving the problem. Others find it most helpful to just go through each of the possible choices, contrasting each as they go along. You should use whatever method feels comfortable and works for you.

While most of these types of questions are not that difficult, we've added a higher percentage of the difficult type, just to give you more practice. Usually there are only one or two questions on this section that contain such subtle distinctions that you're unable to answer confidently. And you then may find yourself stuck deciding between two possible choices, neither of which you're sure about.

EXAMINATION SECTION

TEST 1

DIRECTIONS: The following groups of sentences need to be arranged in an order that makes sense. Select the letter preceding the sequence that represents the BEST sentence order. *PRINT THE LETTER OF THE CORRECT ANSWER IN THE SPACE AT THE RIGHT.*

1.
   I. The keyboard was purposely designed to be a little awkward to slow typists down.
   II. The arrangement of letters on the keyboard of a typewriter was not designed for the convenience of the typist.
   III. Fortunately, no one is suggesting that a new keyboard be designed right away.
   IV. If one were, we would have to learn to type all over again.
   V. The reason was that the early machines were slower than the typists and would jam easily.
   The CORRECT answer is:
   A. I, III, IV, II, V
   B. II, V, I, IV, III
   C. V, I, II, III, IV
   D. II, I, V, III, IV

   1.____

2.
   I. The majority of the new service jobs are part-time or low-paying.
   II. According to the U.S. Bureau of Labor Statistics, jobs in the service sector constitute 72% of all jobs in this country.
   III. If more and more workers receive less and less money, who will buy the goods and services needed to keep the economy going?
   IV. The service sector is by far the fastest growing part of the United States economy.
   V. Some economists look upon this trend with great concern.
   The CORRECT answer is:
   A. II, IV, I, V, III
   B. II, III, IV, I, V
   C. V, IV, II, III, I
   D. III, I, II, IV, V

   2.____

3.
   I. They can also affect one's endurance.
   II. This can stabilize blood sugar levels, and ensure that the brain is receiving a steady, constant, supply of glucose, so that one is *hitting on all cylinders* while taking the test.
   III. By food, we mean real food, not junk food or unhealthy snacks.
   IV. For this reason, it is important not to skip a meal, and to bring food with you to the exam.
   V. One's blood sugar levels can affect how clearly one is able to think and concentrate during an exam.
   The CORRECT answer is:
   A. V, IV, II, III, I
   B. V, II, I, IV, III
   C. V, I, IV, III, II
   D. V, IV, I, III, II

   3.____

4.
I. Those who are the embodiment of desire are absorbed in material quests, and those who are the embodiment of feeling are warriors who value power more than possession.
II. These qualities are in everyone, but in different degrees.
III. But those who value understanding yearn not for goods or victory, but for knowledge.
IV. According to Plato, human behavior flows from three main sources: desire, emotion, and knowledge.
V. In the perfect state, the industrial forces would produce but not rule, the military would protect but not rule, and the forces of knowledge, the philosopher kings, would reign.
The CORRECT answer is:
A. IV, V, I, II, III
B. V, I, II, III, IV
C. IV, III, II, I, V
D. IV, II, I, III, V

5.
I. Of the more than 26,000 tons of garbage produced daily in New York City, 12,000 tons arrive daily at Fresh Kills.
II. In a month, enough garbage accumulates there to fill the Empire State Building.
III. In 1937, the Supreme Court halted the practice of dumping the trash of New York City into the sea.
IV. Although the garbage is compacted, in a few years the mounds of garbage at Fresh Kills will be the highest points south of Maine's Mount Desert Island on the Eastern Seaboard.
V. Instead, tugboats now pull barges of much of the trash to Staten Island and the largest landfill in the world, Fresh Kills.
The CORRECT answer is:
A. III, V, IV, I, II
B. III, V, II, IV, I
C. III, V, I, II, IV
D. III, II, V, IV, I

6.
I. Communists rank equality very high, but freedom very low.
II. Unlike communists, conservatives place a high value on freedom and a very low value on equality.
III. A recent study demonstrated that one way to classify people's political beliefs is to look at the importance placed on two words: freedom and equality.
IV. Thus, by demonstrating how members of these groups feel about the two words, the study has proved to be useful for political analysts in several European countries.
V. According to the study, socialists and liberals rank both freedom and equality very high, while fascists rate both very low.
The CORRECT answer is:
A. III, V, I, II, IV
B. V, IV, III, I, II
C. III, V, IV, II, I
D. III, I, II, IV, V

7. I. "Can there be anything more amazing than this?"
    II. If the riddle is successfully answered, his dead brothers will be brought back to life.
    III. "Even though man sees those around him dying every day," says Dharmaraj, "he still believes and acts as if he were immortal."
    IV. "What is the cause of ceaseless wonder?" asks the Lord of the Lake.
    V. In the ancient epic, The Mahabharata, a riddle is asked of one of the Pandava brothers.

    The CORRECT answer is:
    A. V, II, I, IV, III
    B. V, IV, III, I, II
    C. V, II, IV, III, I
    D. V, II, IV, I, III

8. I. On the contrary, the two main theories—the cooperative (neoclassical) theory and the radical (labor theory)—clearly rest on very different assumptions, which have very different ethical overtones.
    II. The distribution of income is the primary factor in determining the relative levels of material well-being that different groups or individuals attain.
    III. Of all issues in economics, the distribution of income is one of the most controversial.
    IV. The neoclassical theory tends to support the existing income distribution (or minor changes), while the labor theory ends to support substantial changes in the way income is distributed.
    V. The intensity of the controversy reflects the fact that different economic theories are not purely neutral, *detached* theories with no ethical or moral implications.

    The CORRECT answer is:
    A. II, I, V, IV, III
    B. III, II, V, I, IV
    C. III, V, II, I, IV
    D. III, V, IV, I, II

9. I. The pool acts as a broker and ensures that the cheapest power gets used first.
    II. Every six seconds, the pool's computer monitors all of the generating stations in the state and decides which to ask for more power and which to cut back.
    III. The buying and selling of electrical power is handled by the New York Power Pool in Guilderland, New York.
    IV. This is to the advantage of both the buying and selling utilities.
    V. The pool began operation in 1970, and consists of the state's eight electric utilities.

    The CORRECT answer is:
    A. V, I, II, III, IV
    B. IV, II, I, III, V
    C. III, V, I, IV, II
    D. V, III, IV, II, I

10. I. Modern English is much simpler grammatically than Old English.
    II. Finnish grammar is very complicated; there are some fifteen cases, for example.
    III. Chinese, a very old language, may seem to be the exception, but it is the great number of characters/words that must be mastered that makes it so difficult to learn, not its grammar.
    IV. The newest literary language—that is, written as well as spoken—is Finish, whose literary roots go back only to about the middle of the nineteenth century.
    V. Contrary to popular belief, the longer a language is been in use the simpler its grammar—not the reverse.

    The CORRECT answer is:
    A. IV, I, II, III, V
    B. V, I, IV, II, III
    C. I, II, IV, III, V
    D. IV, II, III, I, V

KEY (CORRECT ANSWERS)

1. D
2. A
3. C
4. D
5. C
6. A
7. C
8. B
9. C
10. B

TEST 2

DIRECTIONS: This type of question tests your ability to recognize accurate paraphrasing, well-constructed paragraphs, and appropriate style and tone. It is important that the answer you select contains only the facts or concepts given in the original sentences. It is also important that you be aware of incomplete sentences, inappropriate transitions, unsupported opinions, incorrect usage, and illogical sentence order. Paragraphs that do not include all the necessary facts and concepts, that distort them, or that add new ones are not considered correct.

The format for this section may vary. Sometimes, long paragraphs are given, and emphasis is placed on style and organization. Our first five questions are of this type. Other times, the paragraphs are shorter, and there is less emphasis on style and more emphasis on accurate representation of information. Our second group of five questions are of this nature.

For each of Questions 1 through 10, select the paragraph that BEST expresses the ideas contained in the sentences above it. *PRINT THE LETTER OF THE CORRECT ANSWER IN THE SPACE AT THE RIGHT.*

1.
   I. Listening skills are very important for managers.
   II. Listening skills are not usually emphasized.
   III. Whenever managers are depicted in books, manuals or the media, they are always talking, never listening.
   IV. We'd like you to read the enclosed handout on listening skills and to try to consciously apply them this week.
   V. We guarantee they will improve the quality of your interactions.

   1.____

   A. Unfortunately, listening skills are not usually emphasized for managers. Managers are always depicted as talking, never listening. We'd like you to read the enclosed handout on listening skills. Please try to apply these principles this week. If you do, we guarantee they will improve the quality of your interactions.
   B. The enclosed handout on listening skills will be important improving the quality of your interactions. We guarantee it. All you have to do is take sometime this week to read and to consciously try to apply the principles. Listening skills are very important for manages, but they are not usually emphasized. Whenever managers are depicted in books, manuals or the media, they are always talking, never listening.
   C. Listening well is one of the most important skills a manager can have, yet it's not usually given much attention. Think about any representation of managers in books, manuals, or in the media that you may have seen. They're always talking, never listening. We'd like you to read the enclosed handout on listening skills and consciously try to apply them the rest of the week. We guarantee you will see a difference in the quality of your interactions.

135

D. Effective listening, one very important tool in the effective manager's arsenal, is usually not emphasized enough. The usual depiction of managers in books, manuals or the media is one in which they are always talking, never listening. We'd like you to read the enclosed handout and consciously try to apply the information contained therein throughout the rest of the week. We feel sure that you will see a marked difference in the quality of your interactions.

2.
I. Chekhov wrote three dramatic masterpieces which share certain themes and formats: Uncle Vanya, The Cherry Orchard, and The Three Sisters.
II. They are primarily concerned with the passage of time and how this erodes human aspirations.
III. The plays are haunted by the ghosts of the wasted life.
IV. The characters are concerned with life's lesser problems; however, such as the inability to make decisions, loyalty to the wrong cause, and the inability to be clear.
V. This results in sweet, almost aching, type of a sadness referred to as Chekhovian.

2.____

A. Chekhov wrote three dramatic masterpieces: Uncle Vanya, The Cherry Orchard, and The Three Sisters. These masterpieces share certain themes and formats: the passage of time, how time erodes human aspirations, and the ghosts of wasted life. Each masterpiece is characterized by a sweet, almost aching, type of sadness that has become known as Chekhovian. The sweetness of this sadness hinges on the fact that it is not the great tragedies of life which are destroying these characters, but their minor flaws: indecisiveness, misplaced loyalty, unclarity.
B. The Cherry Orchard, Uncle Vanya, and The Three Sisters are three dramatic masterpieces written by Chekhov that use similar formats to explore a common theme. Each is primarily concerned with the way that passing time wears down human aspirations, and each is haunted by the ghosts of the wasted life. The characters are shown struggling futilely with the lesser problems of life: indecisiveness, loyalty to the wrong cause, and the inability to be clear. These struggles create a mood of sweet, almost aching, sadness that has become known as Chekhovian.
C. Chekhov's dramatic masterpieces are, along with The Cherry Orchard, Uncle Vanya, and The Three Sisters. These plays share certain thematic and formal similarities. They are concerned most of all with the passage of time and the way in which time erodes human aspirations. Each play is haunted by the specter of the wasted life. Chekhov's characters are caught, however, by life's lesser snares: indecisiveness, loyalty to the wrong cause, and unclarity. The characteristic mood is a sweet, almost aching type of sadness that has come to be known as Chekhovian.
D. A Chekhovian mood is characterized by sweet, almost aching, sadness. The term comes from three dramatic tragedies by Chekhov which revolve around the sadness of a wasted life. The three masterpieces (Uncle Vanya, The Three Sisters, and The Cherry Orchard) share the same

theme and format. The plays are concerned with how the passage of time erodes human aspirations. They are peopled with characters who are struggling with life's lesser problems. These are people who are indecisive, loyal to the wrong causes, or are unable to make themselves clear.

3.
I. Movie previews have often helped producers decide which parts of movies they should take out or leave in.
II. The first 1933 preview of King Kong was very helpful to the producers because many people ran screaming from the theater and would not return when four men first attacked by Kong were eaten by giant spiders.
III. The 1950 premiere of Sunset Boulevard resulted in the filming of an entirely new beginning, and a delay of six months in the film's release.
IV. In the original opening scene, William Holden was in a morgue talking with thirty-six other "corpses" about the ways some of them had died.
V. When he began to tell them of his life with Gloria Swanson, the audience found this hilarious, instead of taking the scene seriously.

3.____

A. Movie previews have often helped producers decide what parts of movies they should leave in or take out. For example, the first preview of King Kong in 1933 was very helpful. In one scene, four men were first attacked by Kong and then eaten by giant spiders. Many members of the audience ran screaming from the theater and would not return. The premiere of the 1950 film Sunset Boulevard was also very helpful. In the original opening scene, William Holden was in a morgue with thirty-six other "corpses," discussing the ways some of them had died. When he began to tell them of his life with Gloria Swanson, the audience found this hilarious. They were supposed to take the scene seriously. The result was a delay of six months in the release of the film while a new beginning was added.

B. Movie previews have often helped producers decide whether they should change various parts of a movie. After the 1933 preview of King Kong, a scene in which four men who had been attacked by Kong were eaten by giant spiders was taken out as many people ran screaming from the theater and would not return. The 1950 premiere of Sunset Boulevard also led to some changes. In the original opening scene, William Holden was in a morgue talking with thirty-six other "corpses" about the ways some of them had died. When he began to tell them of his life with Gloria Swanson, the audience found this hilarious, instead of taking the scene seriously.

C. What do Sunset Boulevard and King Kong have in common? Both show the value of using movie previews to test audience reaction. The first 1933 preview of King Kong showed that a scene showing four men being eaten by giant spiders after having been attacked by Kong was too frightening for many people. They ran screaming from the theater and couldn't be coaxed back. The 1950 premiere of Sunset Boulevard was also a scream, but not the kind the producers intended. The movie opens with William Holden lying in a morgue discussing the ways they had died with thirty-six other "corpses." When he began to tell them of his life with Gloria Swanson, the audience couldn't take him seriously. Their laughter caused a six-month delay while the beginning was rewritten.

D. Producers very often use movie previews to decide if changes are needed. The premiere of Sunset Boulevard in 1950 led to a new beginning and a six-month delay in film release. At the beginning, William Holden and thirty-six other "corpses" discuss the ways some of them died. Rather than taking this seriously, the audience thought it was hilarious when he began to tell them of his life with Gloria Swanson. The first 1933 preview of King Kong was very helpful for its producers because one scene so terrified the audience that many of them ran screaming from the theater and would not return. In this particular scene, four men who had first been attacked by Kong were eaten by giant spiders.

4. I. It is common for supervisors to view employees as "things" to be manipulated.
    II. This approach does not motivate employees, nor does the carrot-and-stick approach because employees often recognize these behaviors and resent them.
    III. Supervisors can change these behaviors by using self-inquiry and persistence.
    IV. The best managers genuinely respect those they work with, are supportive and helpful, and are interested in working as a team with those they supervise.
    V. They disagree with the Golden Rule that says "he or she who has the gold makes the rules."

    A. Some managers act as if they think the Golden Rule means "he or she who has the gold makes the rules." They show disrespect to employees by seeing them as "things" to be manipulated. Obviously, this approach does not motivate employees any more than the carrot-and-stick approach motivates them. The employees are smart enough to spot these behaviors and resent them. On the other hand, the managers genuinely respect those they work with, are supportive and helpful, and are interested in working as a team. Self-inquiry and persistence can change even the former type of supervisor into the latter.
    B. Many supervisors all into the trap of viewing employees as "things" to be manipulated, or try to motivate them by using a carrot-and-stick approach. These methods do not motivate employees, who often recognize the behaviors and resent them. Supervisors can change these behaviors, however, by using self-inquiry and persistence. The best managers are supportive and helpful, and have genuine respect for those with whom they work. They are interested in working as a team with those they supervise. To them, the Golden Rule is not "he or she who has the gold makes the rules."
    C. Some supervisors see employees as "things" to be used or manipulated using a carrot-and-stick technique. These methods don't work. Employees often see through them and resent them. A supervisor who

wants to change may do so. The techniques of self-inquiry and persistence can be used to turn him or her into the type of supervisor who doesn't think the Golden Rule is "he or she who has the gold makes the rules." They may become like the best managers who treat those with whom they work with respect and give them help and support. These are the manager who know how to build a team.

D. Unfortunately, many supervisors act as if their employees are objects whose movements they can position at will. This mistaken belief has the same result as another popular motivational technique—the carrot-and-stick approach. Both attitudes can lead to the same result—resentment from those employees who recognize the behaviors for what they are. Supervisors who recognize these behaviors can change through the use of persistence and the use of self-inquiry. It's important to remember that the best managers respect their employees. They readily give necessary help and support and are interested in working as a team with those they supervise. To these managers, the Golden Rule is not "he or she who has the gold makes the rules."

5.
I. The first half of the nineteenth century produced a group of pessimistic poets—Byron, De Musset, Heine, Pushkin, and Leopardi.
II. It also produced a group of pessimistic composers—Schubert, Chopin, Schumann, and even the later Beethoven.
III. Above all, in philosophy, there was the profoundly pessimistic philosopher, Schopenhauer.
IV. The Revolution was dead, the Bourbons were restored, the feudal barons were reclaiming their land, and progress everywhere was being suppressed, as the great age was over.
V. "I thank God," said Goethe, "that I am not young in so thoroughly finished a world."

A. "I thank God," said Goethe, "that I am not young in so thoroughly finished a world." The Revolution was dead, the Bourbons were restored, the feudal barons were reclaiming their land, and progress everywhere was being suppressed. The first half of the nineteenth century produced a group of pessimistic poets: Byron, De Musset, Heine, Pushkin, and Leopardi. It also produced pessimistic composers: Schubert, Chopin, Schumann. Although Beethoven came later, he fits into this group, too. Finally and above all, it also produced a profoundly pessimistic philosopher, Schopenhauer. The great age was over.

B. The first half of the nineteenth century produced a group of pessimistic poets: Byron, De Musset, Heine, Pushkin, and Leopardi. It produced a group of pessimistic composers: Schubert, Chopin, Schumann, and even the later Beethoven. Above all, it produced a profoundly pessimistic philosopher, Schopenhauer. For each of these men, the great age was over. The Revolution was dead, and the Bourbons were restored. The feudal barons were reclaiming their land, and progress everywhere was being suppressed.

5.____

C. The great age was over. The Revolution was dead—the Bourbons were restored, and the feudal barons were reclaiming their land. Progress everywhere was being suppressed. Out of this climate came a profound pessimism. Poets, like Byron, De Musset, Heine, Pushkin, and Leopardi; composers, like Schubert, Chopin, Schumann, and even the later Beethoven; and above all, a profoundly pessimistic philosopher, Schopenauer. This pessimism which arose in the first half of the nineteenth century is illustrated by these words of Goethe, "I thank God that I am not young in so thoroughly finished a world."

D. The first half of the nineteenth century produced a group of pessimistic poets, Byron, De Musset, Heine, Pushkin, and Leopardi—and a group of pessimistic composers, Schubert, Chopin, Schumann, and the later Beethoven. Above it all, it produced a profoundly pessimistic philosopher, Schopenhauer. The great age was over. The Revolution was dead, the Bourbons were restored, the feudal barons were reclaiming their land, and progress everywhere was being suppressed. "I thank God," said Goethe, "that I am not young in so thoroughly finished a world."

6. I. A new manager sometimes may feel insecure about his or her competence in the new position.
   II. The new manager may then exhibit defensive or arrogant behavior towards those one supervises, or the new manager may direct overly flattering behavior toward one's new supervisor.

   A. Sometimes, a new manager may feel insecure about his or her ability to perform well in this new position. The insecurity may lead him or her to treat others differently. He or she may display arrogant or defensive behavior towards those he or she supervises, or be overly flattering to his or her new supervisor.
   B. A new manager may sometimes feel insecure about his or her ability to perform well in the new position. He or she may then become arrogant, defensive, or overly flattering towards those he or she works with.
   C. There are times when a new manager may be insecure about how well he or she can perform in the new job. The new manager may also behave defensive or act in an arrogant way towards those he or she supervises, or overly flatter his or her boss.
   D. Sometimes a new manager may feel insecure about his or her ability to perform well in the new position. He or she may then display arrogant or defensive behavior towards those they supervise, or become overly flattering towards their supervisors.

7. I. It is possible to eliminate unwanted behavior by bringing it under stimulus control—tying the behavior to a cue, and then never, or rarely, giving the cue.
   II. One trainer successfully used this method to keep an energetic young porpoise from coming out of her tank whenever she felt like it, which was potentially dangerous.
   III. Her trainer taught her to do it for a reward, in response to a hand signal, and then rarely gave the signal.

A. Unwanted behavior can be eliminated by tying the behavior to a cue, and then never, or rarely, giving the cue. This is called stimulus control. One trainer was able to use this method to keep an energetic young porpoise from coming out of her tank by teaching her to come out for a reward in response to a hand signal, and then rarely giving the signal.

B. Stimulus control can be used to eliminate unwanted behavior. In this method, behavior is tied to a cue, and then the cue is rarely, if ever, given. One trainer was able to successfully use stimulus control to keep an energetic young porpoise from coming out of her tank whenever she felt like it—a potentially dangerous practice. She taught the porpoise to come out for a reward when she gave a hand signal, and then rarely gave the signal.

C. It is possible to eliminate behavior that is undesirable by bringing it under stimulus control by tying behavior to a signal, and then rarely giving the signal. One trainer successfully used this method to keep an energetic porpoise from coming out of her tank, a potentially dangerous situation. Her trainer taught the porpoise to do it for a reward, in response to a hand signal, and then would rarely give the signal.

D. By using stimulus control, it is possible to eliminate unwanted behavior by tying the behavior to a cue, and then rarely or never give the cue. One trainer was able to use this method to successfully stop a young porpoise from coming out of her tank whenever she felt like it. To curb this potentially dangerous practice, the porpoise was taught by the trainer to come out of the tank for a reward, in response to a hand signal, and then rarely given the signal.

8. I. There is a great deal of concern over the safety of commercial trucks, caused by their greatly increased role in serious accidents since federal deregulation in 1981.
   II. Recently, 60 percent of trucks in New York and Connecticut and 70 percent of trucks in Maryland randomly stopped by state troopers failed safety inspections.
   III. Sixteen states in the United States require no training at all for truck drivers.

   A. Since federal deregulation in 1981, there has been a great deal of concern over the safety of commercial trucks, and their greatly increased role in serious accidents. Recently, 60 percent of trucks in New York and Connecticut, and 70 percent of trucks in Maryland failed safety inspections. Sixteen states in the United States require no training at all for truck drivers.
   B. There is a great deal of concern over the safety of commercial trucks since federal deregulation in 1981. Their role in serious accidents has greatly increased. Recently, 60 percent of trucks randomly stopped in Connecticut and New York and 70 percent in Maryland failed safety inspections conducted by state troopers. Sixteen states in the United States provide no training at all for truck drivers.
   C. Commercial trucks have a greatly increased role in serious accidents since federal deregulation in 1981. This has led to a great deal of concern.

8.____

Recently, 70 percent of trucks in Maryland and 60 percent of trucks in New York and Connecticut failed inspection of those that were randomly stopped by state troopers. Sixteen states in the United States require no training for all truck drivers.

D. Since federal deregulation in 1981, the role that commercial trucks have played in serious accidents has greatly increased, and this has led to a great deal of concern. Recently, 60 percent of trucks in New York and Connecticut, and 70 percent of trucks in Maryland randomly stopped by state troopers failed safety inspections. Sixteen states in the U.S. don't require any training for truck drivers.

9.
I. No matter how much some people have, they still feel unsatisfied and want more, or want to keep what they have forever.
II. One recent television documentary showed several people flying from New York to Paris for a one-day shopping spree to buy platinum earrings, because they were bored.
III. In Brazil, some people were ordering coffins that cost a minimum of $45,000 and are equipping them with deluxe stereos, televisions, and other graveyard necessities.

9.____

A. Some people, despite having a great deal, still feel unsatisfied and want more, or think they can keep what they have forever. One recent documentary on television showed several people enroute from Paris to New York for a one day shopping spree to buy platinum earrings, because they were bored. Some people in Brazil are even ordering coffins equipped with such graveyard necessities as deluxe stereos and televisions. The price of the coffins start at $45,000.
B. No matter how much some people have, they may feel unsatisfied. This leads them to want more, or to want to keep what they have forever. Recently, a television documentary depicting several people flying from New York to Paris for a one day shopping spree to buy platinum earrings. They were bored. Some people in Brazil are ordering coffins that cost at least $45,000 and come equipped with deluxe televisions, stereos and other necessary graveyard items.
C. Some people will be dissatisfied no matter how much they have. They may want more, or they may want to keep what they have forever. One recent television documentary showed several people, motivated by boredom, jetting from New York to Paris for a one-day shopping spree to buy platinum earrings. In Brazil, some people are ordering coffins equipped with deluxe stereos, televisions and other graveyard necessities. The minimum price for these coffins—$45,000.
D. Some people are never satisfied. No matter how much they have they still want more, or think they can keep what they have forever. One television documentary recently showed several people flying from New York to Paris for the day to buy platinum earrings because they were bored. In Brazil, some people are ordering coffins that cost $45,000 and are equipped with deluxe stereos, televisions and other graveyard necessities.

10.
I. A television signal or video signal has three parts.
II. Its parts are the black-and-white portion, the color portion, and the synchronizing (sync) pulses, which keep the picture stable.
III. Each video source, whether it's a camera or a video-cassette recorder contains its own generator of these synchronizing pulses to accompany the picture that it's sending in order to keep it steady and straight.
IV. In order to produce a clean recording, a video-cassette recorder must "lock-up" to the sync pulses that are part of the video it is trying to record, and this effort may be very noticeable if the device does not have gunlock.

10.____

A. There are three parts to a television or video signal: the black-and-white part, the color part, and the synchronizing (sync) pulses, which keep the picture stable. Whether it's a video-cassette recorder or a camera, each video source contains its own pulse that synchronizes and generates the picture it's sending in order to keep it straight and steady. A video-cassette recorder must "lock up" to the sync pulses that are part of the video it's trying to record. If the device doesn't have gunlock, this effort must be very noticeable.
B. A video signal or television is comprised of three parts: the black-and-white portion, the color portion, and the sync (synchronizing) pulses, which keep the picture stable. Whether it's a camera or a video-cassette recorder, each video source contains its own generator of these synchronizing pulses. These accompany the picture that it's sending in order to keep it straight and steady. A video-cassette recorder must "lock up" to the sync pulses that are part of the video it is trying to record in order to produce a clean recording. This effort may be very noticeable if the device does not have gunlock.
C. There are three parts to a television or video signal: the color portion, the black-and-white portion, and the sync (synchronizing pulses). These keep the picture stable. Each video source, whether it's a video-cassette recorder or a camera, generates these synchronizing pulses accompanying the picture it's sending in order to keep it straight and steady. If a clean recording is to be produced, a video-cassette recorder must store the sync pulses that are part of the video it is trying to record. This effort may not be noticeable if the device does not have gunlock.
D. A television signal or video signal has three parts: the black-and-white portion, the color portion, and the synchronizing (sync) pulses. It's the sync pulses which keep the picture stable, which accompany it and keep it steady and straight. Whether it's a camera or a video-cassette recorder, each video source contains its own generator of these synchronizing pulses. To produce a clean recording, a video-cassette recorder must "lock up" to the sync pulses that are part of the video it is trying to record. If the device does not have gunlock, this effort may be very noticeable.

KEY (CORRECT ANSWERS)

1. C
2. B
3. A
4. B
5. D
6. A
7. B
8. D
9. C
10. D

PREPARING WRITTEN MATERIAL
EXAMINATION SECTION
TEST 1

DIRECTIONS: Each of the sentences in this test may be classified under one of the following four categories:
- A. Faulty because of incorrect grammar or word usage
- B. Faulty because of incorrect punctuation
- C. Faulty because of incorrect capitalization or incorrect spelling
- D. Correct

Examine each sentence carefully to determine under which of the above four options it is best classified. Then, in the space to the right, print the capital letter preceding the option which is the BEST of the four suggested above. (Note that each faulty sentence contains but one type of error. Consider a sentence to be correct if it contains none of the types of errors mentioned, even though there may be other correct ways of expressing the same thought.)

1. He sent the notice to the clerk who you hired yesterday. 1.____

2. It must be admitted, however that you were not informed of this change. 2.____

3. Only the employee who have served in this grade for at least two years are eligible for promotion. 3.____

4. The work was divided equally between she and Mary. 4.____

5. He thought that you were not available at that time. 5.____

6. When the messenger returns; please give him this package. 6.____

7. The new secretary prepared, typed, addressed, and delivered, the notices. 7.____

8. Walking into the room, his desk can be seen at the rear. 8.____

9. Although John has worked here longer than She, he produces a smaller amount of work. 9.____

10. She said she could of typed this report yesterday. 10.____

11. Neither one of these procedures are adequate for the efficient performance of this task. 11.____

12. The typewriter is the tool of the typist; the cash register, the tool of the cashier. 12.____

13. "The assignment must be completed as soon as possible" said the supervisor. 13._____

14. As you know, office handbooks are issued to all new Employees. 14._____

15. Writing a speech is sometimes easier than to deliver it before an audience. 15._____

16. Mr. Brown our accountant, will audit the accounts next week. 16._____

17. Give the assignment to whomever is able to do it most efficiently. 17._____

18. The supervisor expected either your or I to file these reports. 18._____

KEY (CORRECT ANSWERS)

1.	A	11.	A
2.	B	12.	C
3.	D	13.	B
4.	A	14.	C
5.	D	15.	A
6.	B	16.	B
7.	B	17.	A
8.	A	18.	A
9.	C		
10.	A		

TEST 2

DIRECTIONS: Each of the sentences in this test may be classified under one of the following four categories:
- A. Faulty because of incorrect grammar or word usage
- B. Faulty because of incorrect punctuation
- C. Faulty because of incorrect capitalization or incorrect spelling
- D. Correct

Examine each sentence carefully to determine under which of the above four options it is best classified. Then, in the space to the right, print the capital letter preceding the option which is the BEST of the four suggested above. (Note that each faulty sentence contains but one type of error. Consider a sentence to be correct if it contains none of the types of errors mentioned, even though there may be other correct ways of expressing the same thought.)

1. The fire apparently started in the storeroom, which is usually locked.   1.____
2. On approaching the victim, two bruises were noticed by this officer.   2.____
3. The officer, who was there examined the report with great care.   3.____
4. Each employee in the office had a seperate desk.   4.____
5. All employees including members of the clerical staff, were invited to the lecture. 5.____
6. The suggested Procedure is similar to the one now in use.   6.____
7. No one was more pleased with the new procedure than the chauffeur.   7.____
8. He tried to persaude her to change the procedure.   8.____
9. The total of the expenses charged to petty cash were high.   9.____
10. An understanding between him and I was finally reached.   10.____

KEY (CORRECT ANSWERS)

1.	D	6.	C
2.	A	7.	D
3.	B	8.	C
4.	C	9.	A
5.	B	10.	A

TEST 3

DIRECTIONS: Each of the sentences in this test may be classified under one of the following four categories:
- A. Faulty because of incorrect grammar or word usage
- B. Faulty because of incorrect punctuation
- C. Faulty because of incorrect capitalization or incorrect spelling
- D. Correct

Examine each sentence carefully to determine under which of the above four options it is best classified. Then, in the space to the right, print the capital letter preceding the option which is the BEST of the four suggested above. (Note that each faulty sentence contains but one type of error. Consider a sentence to be correct if it contains none of the types of errors mentioned, even though there may be other correct ways of expressing the same thought.)

1. They told both he and I that the prisoner had escaped. 1.____

2. Any superior officer, who, disregards the just complaint of his subordinates, is remiss in the performance of his duty. 2.____

3. Only those members of the national organization who resided in the Middle West attended the conference in Chicago. 3.____

4. We told him to give the national organization assignment to whoever was available. 4.____

5. Please do not disappoint and embarass us by not appearing in court. 5.____

6. Although the office's speech proved to be entertaining, the topic was not relevent to the main theme of the conference. 6.____

7. In February all new officers attended a training course in which they were learned in their principal duties and the fundamental operating procedure of the department. 7.____

8. I personally seen inmate Jones threaten inmates Smith and Green with bodily harm if they refused to participate in the plot. 8.____

9. To the layman, who on a chance visit to the prison observes everything functioning smoothly, the maintenance of prison discipline may seem to be a relatively easily realizable objective. 9.____

10. The prisoners in cell block fourty were forbidden to sit on the cell cots during the recreation hour. 10.____

KEY (CORRECT ANSWERS)

1. A 6. C
2. B 7. A
3. C 8. A
4. D 9. D
5. C 10. C

———

TEST 4

DIRECTIONS: Each of the sentences in this test may be classified under one of the following four categories:
- A. Faulty because of incorrect grammar or word usage
- B. Faulty because of incorrect punctuation
- C. Faulty because of incorrect capitalization or incorrect spelling
- D. Correct

Examine each sentence carefully to determine under which of the above four options it is best classified. Then, in the space to the right, print the capital letter preceding the option which is the BEST of the four suggested above. (Note that each faulty sentence contains but one type of error. Consider a sentence to be correct if it contains none of the types of errors mentioned, even though there may be other correct ways of expressing the same thought.)

1. I cannot encourage you any.   1._____
2. You always look well in those sort of clothes.   2._____
3. Shall we go to the park?   3._____
4. The man whome he introduced was Mr. Carey.   4._____
5. She saw the letter laying here this morning.   5._____
6. It should rain before the Afternoon is over.   6._____
7. They have already went home.   7._____
8. That Jackson will be elected is evident.   8._____
9. He does not hardly approve of us.   9._____
10. It was he, who won the prize.   10._____

KEY (CORRECT ANSWERS)

1.	A	6.	C
2.	A	7.	A
3.	D	8.	D
4.	C	9.	A
5.	A	10.	B

TEST 5

DIRECTIONS: Each of the sentences in this test may be classified under one of the following four categories:
    A. Faulty because of incorrect grammar or word usage
    B. Faulty because of incorrect punctuation
    C. Faulty because of incorrect capitalization or incorrect spelling
    D. Correct

Examine each sentence carefully to determine under which of the above four options it is best classified. Then, in the space to the right, print the capital letter preceding the option which is the BEST of the four suggested above. (Note that each faulty sentence contains but one type of error. Consider a sentence to be correct if it contains none of the types of errors mentioned, even though there may be other correct ways of expressing the same thought.)

1. Shall we go to the park.   1.____
2. They are, alike, in this particular way.   2.____
3. They gave the poor man sume food when he knocked on the door.   3.____
4. I regret the loss caused by the error.   4.____
5. The students' will have a new teacher.   5.____
6. They sweared to bring out all the facts.   6.____
7. He decided to open a branch store on 33rd street.   7.____
8. His speed is equal and more than that of a racehorse.   8.____
9. He felt very warm on that Summer day.   9.____
10. He was assisted by his friend, who lives in the next house.   10.____

KEY (CORRECT ANSWERS)

1.	B	6.	A
2.	B	7.	C
3.	C	8.	A
4.	D	9.	C
5.	B	10.	D

TEST 6

DIRECTIONS: Each of the sentences in this test may be classified under one of the following four categories:
- A. Faulty because of incorrect grammar or word usage
- B. Faulty because of incorrect punctuation
- C. Faulty because of incorrect capitalization or incorrect spelling
- D. Correct

Examine each sentence carefully to determine under which of the above four options it is best classified. Then, in the space to the right, print the capital letter preceding the option which is the BEST of the four suggested above. (Note that each faulty sentence contains but one type of error. Consider a sentence to be correct if it contains none of the types of errors mentioned, even though there may be other correct ways of expressing the same thought.)

1. The climate of New York is colder than California. 1._____
2. I shall wait for you on the corner. 2._____
3. Did we see the boy who, we think, is the leader. 3._____
4. Being a modest person, John seldom talks about his invention. 4._____
5. The gang is called the smith street bos. 5._____
6. He seen the man break into the store. 6._____
7. We expected to lay still there for quite a while. 7._____
8. He is considered to be the Leader of his organization. 8._____
9. Although I recieved an invitation, I won't go. 9._____
10. The letter must be here some place. 10._____

KEY (CORRECT ANSWERS)

1.	A	6.	A
2.	D	7.	A
3.	B	8.	C
4.	D	9.	C
5.	C	10.	A

TEST 7

DIRECTIONS: Each of the sentences in this test may be classified under one of the following four categories:
- A. Faulty because of incorrect grammar or word usage
- B. Faulty because of incorrect punctuation
- C. Faulty because of incorrect capitalization or incorrect spelling
- D. Correct

Examine each sentence carefully to determine under which of the above four options it is best classified. Then, in the space to the right, print the capital letter preceding the option which is the BEST of the four suggested above. (Note that each faulty sentence contains but one type of error. Consider a sentence to be correct if it contains none of the types of errors mentioned, even though there may be other correct ways of expressing the same thought.)

1. I though it to be he.   1.____
2. We expect to remain here for a long time.   2.____
3. The committee was agreed.   3.____
4. Two-thirds of the building are finished.   4.____
5. The water was froze.   5.____
6. Everyone of the salesmen must supply their own car.   6.____
7. Who is the author of Gone With the Wind?   7.____
8. He marched on and declaring that he would never surrender.   8.____
9. Who shall I say called?   9.____
10. Everyone has left but they.   10.____

KEY (CORRECT ANSWERS)

1.	A	6.	A
2.	D	7.	B
3.	D	8.	A
4.	A	9.	D
5.	A	10.	D

TEST 8

DIRECTIONS: Each of the sentences in this test may be classified under one of the following four categories:
- A. Faulty because of incorrect grammar or word usage
- B. Faulty because of incorrect punctuation
- C. Faulty because of incorrect capitalization or incorrect spelling
- D. Correct

Examine each sentence carefully to determine under which of the above four options it is best classified. Then, in the space to the right, print the capital letter preceding the option which is the BEST of the four suggested above. (Note that each faulty sentence contains but one type of error. Consider a sentence to be correct if it contains none of the types of errors mentioned, even though there may be other correct ways of expressing the same thought.)

1. Who did we give the order to? 1._____
2. Send your order in immediately. 2._____
3. I believe I paid the Bill. 3._____
4. I have not met but one person. 4._____
5. Why aren't Tom, and Fred, going to the dance? 5._____
6. What reason is there for him not going? 6._____
7. The seige of Malta was a tremendous event. 7._____
8. I was there yesterday I assure you 8._____
9. Your ukulele is better than mine. 9._____
10. No one was there only Mary. 10._____

KEY (CORRECT ANSWERS)

1.	A	6.	A
2.	D	7.	C
3.	C	8.	B
4.	A	9.	C
5.	B	10.	A

TEST 9

DIRECTIONS: In each of the following groups of sentences, one of the four sentences is faulty in grammar, punctuation, or capitalization. Select the INCORRECT sentence in each case.

1. A. If you had stood at home and done your homework, you would not have failed in arithmetic.
    B. Her affected manner annoyed every member of the audience.
    C. How will the new law affect our income taxes?
    D. The plants were not affected by the long, cold winter, but they succumbed to the drought of summer.

    1.____

2. A. He is one of the most able men who have been in the Senate.
    B. It is he who is to blame for the lamentable mistake.
    C. Haven't you a helpful suggestion to make at this time?
    D. The money was robbed from the blind man's cup.

    2.____

3. A. The amount of children in this school is steadily increasing.
    B. After taking an apple from the table, she went out to play.
    C. He borrowed a dollar from me.
    D. I had hoped my brother would arrive before me.

    3.____

4. A. Whom do you think I hear from every week?
    B. Who do you think is the right man for the job?
    C. Who do you think I found in the room?
    D. He is the man whom we considered a good candidate for the presidency.

    4.____

5. A. Quietly the puppy laid down before the fireplace.
    B. You have made your bed; now lie in it.
    C. I was badly sunburned because I had lain too long in the sun.
    D. I laid the doll on the bed and left the room.

    5.____

KEY (CORRECT ANSWERS)

1. A
2. D
3. A
4. C
5. A